The Shakespeare Handbooks

THE SHAKESPEARE HANDBOOKS

Series Editor: John Russell Brown

PUBLISHED

John Russell Brown	*Hamlet*
John Russell Brown	*Macbeth*
Paul Edmondson	*Twelfth Night*
Bridget Escolme	*Antony and Cleopatra*
Margaret Jane Kidnie	*The Taming of the Shrew*
Christopher McCullough	*The Merchant of Venice*
Paul Prescott	*Richard III*
Lesley Wade Soule	*As You Like It*

FORTHCOMING

Roger Apfelbaum	*Much Ado About Nothing*
David Carnegie	*Julius Caesar*
Kevin Ewert	*Henry V*
Trevor Griffiths	*The Tempest*
Stuart Hampton-Reeves	*Measure for Measure*
Edward L. Rocklin	*Romeo and Juliet*
Martin White	*A Midsummer Night's Dream*

The Shakespeare Handbooks

The Taming of the Shrew

Margaret Jane Kidnie

palgrave
macmillan

First published 2006 by
PALGRAVE MACMILLAN
Houndmills, Basingstoke, Hampshire RG21 6XS and
175 Fifth Avenue, New York, N.Y. 10010
Companies and representatives throughout the world

PALGRAVE MACMILLAN is the global academic imprint of the Palgrave Macmillan division of St. Martin's Press, LLC and of Palgrave Macmillan Ltd. Macmillan® is a registered trademark in the United States, United Kingdom and other countries. Palgrave is a registered trademark in the European Union and other countries.

ISBN-13: 978–1–4039–4539–6 hardback
ISBN-10: 1–4039–4539–X   hardback
ISBN-13: 978–1–4039–4540–2 paperback
ISBN-10: 1–4039–4540–3   paperback

This book is printed on paper suitable for recycling and made from fully managed and sustained forest sources.

A catalogue record for this book is available from the British Library.

A catalog record for this book is available from the Library of Congress

10   9   8   7   6   5   4   3   2   1
15   14   13   12   11   10   09   08   07   06

Printed in China

For Madelyn, Thomas, and Connor

Contents

General Editor's Preface

The Shakespeare Handbooks provide an innovative way of studying the theatrical life of the plays. The commentaries, which are their core feature, enable a reader to envisage the words of a text unfurling in performance, involving actions and meanings not readily perceived except in rehearsal or performance. The aim is to present the plays in the environment for which they were written and to offer an experience as close as possible to an audience's progressive experience of a production.

While each book has the same range of contents, their authors have been encouraged to shape them according to their own critical and scholarly understanding and their first-hand experience of theatre practice. The various chapters are designed to complement the commentaries: the cultural context of each play is presented together with quotations from original sources; the authority of its text or texts is considered with what is known of the earliest performances; key performances and productions of its subsequent stage history are both described and compared. The aim in all this has been to help readers to develop their own informed and imaginative view of a play in ways that supplement the provision of standard editions and are more user-friendly than detailed stage histories or collections of criticism from diverse sources.

Further volumes are in preparation so that, within a few years, the Shakespeare Handbooks will be available for all the plays that are frequently studied and performed.

John Russell Brown

Preface

The Taming of the Shrew (*The Shrew*) has come to seem one of Shakespeare's most difficult comedies. Even the precise shape of the text is open to interpretation, with some scholars advocating as Shakespearean the more extensive Christopher Sly scenes found in an anonymous 1594 version of the play. The more pressing debate, of course, centres on how to interpret the gender politics of a comedy that dramatizes a woman married against her will and 'tamed' by her husband.

Critics over the years have justified – and refused to justify – Shakespeare's action by situating the taming plot within a wide range of interpretative approaches. The play's fortunes in the theatre and on film have proven no less varied or controversial. Played in the Restoration and through to the nineteenth century as slapstick farce, *The Shrew* came to seem in twentieth-century performance something rather more serious. Whether Katherina's final speech insisting on a wife's subjection and due obedience to her husband seemed motivated by a sincere belief in the value of hierarchical gender roles within marriage, or by vicious abuse at the hands of her husband, the trajectory of the taming plot was no longer so easily bracketed off as a bit of rough-house fun.

This book offers a performance-oriented introduction to *The Shrew*. A detailed commentary in Chapter 2, keyed to the New Penguin Shakespeare (ed. G. R. Hibbard, 1968), is cross-referenced to 'Key Productions and Performances' in Chapter 4. This section documents the specific choices made by five stage and film productions, illustrating the wide range of critical and political response this play has found in performance. These chapters are complemented by analyses of the 'Text and Early Performances' (Chapter 1) and an assessment of the play's critical heritage. The purpose of this book is not just, or even primarily, to widen the reader's knowledge of performance choices made by past productions. Rather, its goal is to encourage readers to assess competing interpretative choices for themselves, and to provide them with the tools that will allow them to draw on critical and theatrical traditions as springboards to their own imagined stagings of this challenging play.

This book has benefited immensely from the ready support and apt guidance of the series general editor, John Russell Brown. At Palgrave Macmillan, Sonya Barker and Valery Rose made valuable suggestions concerning both content and design, and from beginning to end Kate Wallis was the immensely capable and supportive editor every author dreams of encountering. James Purkis read and commented on the typescript, and his excellent feedback was taken up rather more often than I care to admit.

M.J.K.

1 *The Text and Early Performances*

The Taming of the Shrew (*The Shrew*), performed sometime in the 1590s, was probably one of Shakespeare's first attempts at writing for the stage. The earliest surviving edition of the play was published in 1623, seven years after Shakespeare's death, as part of an expensive and prestigious collection of 36 plays called *Mr William Shakespeares Comedies, Histories, & Tragedies*. The volume was printed in folio (a printing term that means that each sheet of paper was folded only once), and scholars distinguish this collection from other, later editions of the complete works by calling it the First Folio. All subsequent editions of *The Shrew* derive, ultimately, from the text as printed in the First Folio.

This straightforward publication history is troubled, however, by the existence of a comedy published anonymously in 1594 called *The Taming of a Shrew* (*A Shrew*). Not only are the titles of these plays nearly identical but, in distinction to other shrew-taming dramas of the sixteenth century, each weaves together three separate storylines involving a commoner called Sly who is imposed on to believe he is a lord, an unruly elder daughter who is 'tamed' by her new husband, and a subplot in which her obedient younger sister(s) deceive(s) their father to marry for love. It seems almost impossible that these two similarly structured plays could have been written entirely independently of one another, and yet the many differences between them prevent scholars from identifying *The Shrew* and *A Shrew* as different editions of the same play. *A Shrew* is much shorter (just over half the length) of *The Shrew*; it relocates the action from Padua to Athens, and renames all of the characters except Sly and Katherina; it simplifies the action of the subplot by leaving out the pantaloon figure of Gremio and providing Katherina with two younger sisters, thus omitting any rivalry among suitors and the need for complicated disguises; and it sustains the Sly framing device through to the end of the play, rather than abandoning it after Act I, scene i. The relation between these two plays is one of the most enduring problems of Shakespearean textual scholarship.

The various theories that have been devised to explain the provenance of *The/A Shrew*, and the similarities and differences between them, are usually divided into three broad groups. The first possibility, one that dominated Shakespearean textual studies until the early years of the twentieth century, is that *A Shrew* is a source-text: Shakespeare revised somebody else's play, making fairly minor changes to the taming plot, trimming the Sly material, and substantially reworking the subplot. There are two potential problems with this idea. First, both plays evidently derive from Ariosto's *I Suppositi* (translated into English by George Gascoigne in 1566 as *Supposes*), and Shakespeare's version follows the complications of Ariosto's plot more closely. Shakespeare, admittedly, might have taken up the story of *A Shrew* and found a way to build into his adopted narrative Ariosto's master–servant disguises, but this scenario still fails to account for a second problem, which is that *A Shrew* seems to garble passages in *The Shrew*. Scholars cite a number of passages to argue for the textual dependence of *A Shrew* on *The Shrew*. The best example occurs during the tailor's scene when Katherina, in Shakespeare's version, says 'I'll have no bigger. This doth fit the time, / And gentlewomen wear such caps as these', and Petruchio, picking up on 'gentlewomen' and punning on 'gentle' to mean both 'of the gentry' and 'mild', replies, 'When you are gentle, you shall have one too, / And not till then' (IV.iii.69–72). *A Shrew* provides a line that approximates Petruchio's reply – 'Ay, when you're meek and gentle but not before' – but the pun on 'gentle' is lost, since Katherina's initial remark makes no mention of 'gentlewomen': 'Thou shalt not keep me nor feed me as thou list, / For I will home again unto my father's house'. Both versions of this exchange, one should note, make good sense. The argument is simply that comparison suggests places where *A Shrew* evidently picks up on a word or turn of phrase found in *The Shrew*, but fails to capitalize fully on the wordplay or pun. For many critics this is suggestive, not of Shakespeare improving an existing play, but of the corruption of Shakespeare's play.

A perception that *A Shrew* (badly) replicates *The Shrew* motivates a second explanation: that the anonymous play is a memorial reconstruction. As the label suggests, this argument is that the garbled passages, awkward repetitions, and insertion of lines from the plays of Christopher Marlowe (*Tamburlaine* and *Dr Faustus*, in particular), are signs that *A Shrew* was prepared by a compiler seeking to reassemble Shakespeare's play from memory or notes. This theory runs into trouble when it tries to account for the differences between the two plays. The disparities, particularly around the subplot, seem too great to be able to trace a straight line from *The Shrew* to *A Shrew*. If the compiler was trying to reproduce *The Shrew*, how did he (or they) get the subplot so wrong, and yet manage to produce a playable story? And where did the extra Sly material come from? Advocates of memorial reconstruction argue either that the compiler simply made the best of a bad thing, or that he was remembering a slightly different version than the text that survives in *The Shrew* – a version either written by Shakespeare or adapted by somebody else.

A third possibility is that both *A Shrew* and *The Shrew* imperfectly reproduce a lost Shakespearean original. In this configuration of the evidence, *A Shrew* remains a corrupt memorial reconstruction, while *The Shrew* is incomplete insofar as it fails to include all the Sly passages. This theory has found some support, mainly because readers of the Folio wonder why Sly has no further lines after a stage direction at the end of Act I, scene i cues him and his company to 'sit and mark' (l. 251). A perception that Shakespeare's Sly plot as preserved in the Folio is corrupt is only reinforced by an awareness that a fuller version survives in *A Shrew*. Some scholars speculate that the Sly material in *A Shrew* might indeed be Shakespearean, omitted from *The Shrew* either by mistake (accidentally lost in, or on the way to, the printing-house) or cut merely to serve the purposes of a particular performance. The terrain, however, is treacherous, with arguments both for and against the existence of a now-lost epilogue in Shakespeare's version of the play turning on, as Richard Hosley explains, a question of aesthetics: 'In the critic's judgment would *The Shrew* be a better play if it had a dramatic epilogue?' (1961, p. 19). Alexander Pope incorporated the Sly passages into the Folio text in his edition of 1720–5, a practice that was followed by editors throughout most of the eighteenth century. Since Edmond Malone's edition of 1790 these scenes have usually been relegated to appendices.

They continue, however, to have a vital stage life, which in part explains why critical and theatrical explorations of *The Shrew* often lead, at some point, to *A Shrew* and its potential relation to Shakespeare's play. Because the evidence on which scholars rely consists almost entirely of analyses of similarities and differences between the two texts, the arguments in favour of one or other theory (source-text, memorial reconstruction, lost original) fluctuate according to dominant interpretative trends. In a modern context in which scholars are sceptical about our ability to reconstruct history in anything but our own critical image, and are reluctant to assign relative 'value' to different texts, the trend is towards studying these two plays as independent theatrical documents. Each is interesting in its own right and offers a key intertext for the other – an importance which is not limited simply to what we may, or may not, be able to infer about Shakespeare's involvement.

The title-page to the 1594 edition of *A Shrew* tells us that this is the text 'As it was sundry times acted by the *Right honorable the Earle of* Pembrook his seruants'. A note in Henslowe's diary of a performance of 'the tamyng of A shrowe' at Newington Butts on 11 June 1594 suggests that the Chamberlain's Men (Shakespeare's company) also had access to a version of the play. The printing rights to *A Shrew* were transferred from Nicholas Ling to John Smethwick in 1607, but when Smethwick reprinted the play in quarto in 1631, it was *The Shrew*, not *A Shrew*, that he published. Both Pembroke's Men and the Chamberlain's Men seem to have had a Shrew play in their repertoire by 1594, but we cannot recover for certain whether this was the same play, perhaps cut differently for performance, or two different plays. A theatrical company usually had exclusive access to a playtext, but it was not unheard of for players to commission a new drama on a popular subject-matter (we know, for instance, that Ben Jonson wrote a play called *Richard Crookback* in response to Shakespeare's success with the historical material surrounding the reign of Richard III). As far as the legal situation concerning print publication goes, the example of Smethwick suggests that having printing rights to *A*

Shrew also gave one rights to *The Shrew*. The textual complications and evident fluidity between these (very slightly) differently titled plays in the late sixteenth and early seventeenth centuries mean that it is impossible to determine with certainty how many Shrew plays were in circulation, whether they were recognized at the time as distinct plays, and what exactly was performed on stage in Shakespeare's day.

Discussion of the earliest performances of *The/A Shrew* is, therefore, extremely speculative. By setting what we know about early modern theatrical conventions and the construction of the amphitheatres alongside certain peculiarities of the Folio text of *The Shrew* one may at least begin to suggest, if not what was actually performed, then at least how players might have set about staging this text. The play was almost certainly staged in a circular theatre that, like the Globe, was in the open air. A thrust stage was surrounded on three sides by a yard to hold standing spectators and behind the yard there would be tiered galleries for seated spectators. The stage (but not the yard) was protected from the elements by a roof supported by two pillars, downstage left and right. There were no sets to indicate location, and since the performance was open air, there were also no lighting changes.

An audience's sense of location therefore depended on costume, a few basic properties that could be carried on and off the stage with ease and, most importantly, the characters' dialogue. The two opening narrative speeches of Act I.i serve in classic fashion the function of exposition (ll. 1–45). The name of the first speaker's companion is introduced (Tranio), a hierarchical relationship between them is established (Tranio is the 'trusty servant' to his 'gentle master'), the action is set in 'fair Padua' (in contrast to the location of the Sly narrative in rural England), and these characters are given motivation – Lucentio has travelled from his home in Pisa, with his father's blessing, to study virtue. These verbal details, in a manner not entirely dissimilar to the way establishing shots in modern films serve to orient viewers geographically and temporally, create a sense of place on the bare early modern stage. Likewise, references to the 'home' of Grumio and Petruchio throughout Act IV, scene i make it clear that the action has shifted from Padua, the home of Baptista and his daughters, to Verona. In the earliest performances, this scene change would have been visually indicated through the introduction of a new set of characters (Curtis, Nathaniel, Philip, and the others), perhaps wearing a distinctive style of livery or uniform, and perhaps bringing on stage a table and chairs to suggest the particular features of this new location (IV.i.1–10).

This is not to say, however, that a specific location is always imagined, or even necessary. The lack of extensive stage sets allowed for a far freer manipulation of place, and in many instances the action remains unlocalized, without a fixed or carefully demarcated setting. Bianca's lessons in Latin and music (Act III, scene i), for example, might take place in a garden, a drawing room, or in her 'closet' or private chambers, but as there are no indicators of place suggested in the language, it is probably most accurate to suggest that in Shakespeare's theatre the scene simply took place on a bare stage. Certain theatrical conventions surrounding costume could also help to create, if not location, then at least a sense of situation and context. The Pedant is described in IV.iv as entering 'drest like Vincentio', and the Folio further clarifies a few lines later that he is 'booted and bare headed' (ll. 1–17). This costuming information is significant because, in accordance with the conventions of Shakespeare's stage, it indicates that this character has been travelling (hence the boots), and shows polite deference to Baptista by removing his hat when Baptista enters. A modern production may choose to follow these directions, but the problem with stage conventions is that they rely for meaning on a shared historical and cultural context – they convey meaning, in other words, only within a signifying system understood by both actors and their audiences. The implication for an early modern audience of a character entering in boots will probably be lost to modern spectators more accustomed to travelling by car, train and airplane than by horseback, and for whom a more instantly meaningful theatrical sign for 'travel' would be a suitcase.

A major, and still unresolved, question surrounding the earliest performances of *The Shrew* concerns stage space. At the beginning of the second induction, Sly and his attendants are told in the Folio to enter 'aloft'. The most obvious explanation of this fairly common direction is that the actors were to perform this scene in the small playing space above and behind the main stage (the same space that probably served a few years later as Juliet's balcony). Some theatre historians, however, consider this area too small to hold comfortably as many as six actors (Sly, the lord, the Page, and perhaps three other servingmen), and note in addition that, tucked away at the back of the stage, the actors would have a problem being seen and heard. The direction at the end of the second induction is that these actors 'Sit and mark'. It seems strange for this number of actors to stay onstage, without lines, through the whole performance, and it seems at least possible that they either slipped away or invented business for themselves. Another potential problem with this staging, if we assume that Sly and the others remained onstage to watch the play to the end, is that this balcony would no longer be available to double as the musicians' gallery. The Folio notes specifically that '*Music plays*' when Katherina and Petruchio return from the church in Act III, scene ii. If they were unable to play from the gallery, the musicians may have instead entered the stage with the wedding party and its guests.

Exactly how the Sly scenes were staged in the early modern amphitheatres necessarily remains hypothetical, particularly when one considers their uncertain textual provenance – did Sly's part indeed end after Act I, scene i, or continue to the end of the play as indicated in *A Shrew*? Or something else altogether? If one assumes that Sly was onstage at least until the end of Act 1, scene i, stage space becomes a pressing problem when the action moves from the Inductions into the Padua action. By the time Baptista, his daughters and their suitors enter at I.i.46, there are three distinct groups of characters onstage: the Paduans (Baptista and the others), the visiting Pisans (Lucentio and Tranio), and the onstage spectators (Sly and his attendants). The size of the stage varied from one amphitheatre to another, but it was never huge. The question is how the actors might have blocked the scene in order to sustain the pretence that the entering Paduans fail to notice or hear the two Pisans, for both of these groups not to trip over Sly, and for a theatre audience to see all three groups (always remembering that there were spectators surrounding the stage on three sides). The clear benefit of situating Sly's group in the gallery above and behind the stage is that it frees the main playing area for the performance of the play within the play (the action involving Baptista and his two daughters), while providing Sly a vantage-point from which to watch and comment. With Sly's group out of the way, one can imagine Lucentio and Tranio simply standing aside upon the entrance of the others, or even concealing their presence behind one or both of the two large pillars downstage left and right.

Perhaps, however, it is a mistake to assume that Shakespeare's actors took the trouble to make sure that sightlines were always clear, and perhaps audiences came to the theatre as much to hear a play as to see it. What seems commonsense to actors and theatre historians now, may not have been self-evident to a playing company at the end of the sixteenth century. That said, the shape and construction of the stage on which the show is performed will always, to some extent, determine the options available to actors. Soliloquies in a modern darkened theatre often create the effect of a character thinking out loud, and seem to imply privileged insight into a character's true thoughts; in contrast to the interpretative scope available in dialogue, the assumption is that soliloquising characters never lie. While this type of interiority was available on Shakespeare's stage, an open-air theatre allows for a freer exchange between actors and audience, and this dynamic might more readily encourage an actor to break the dramatic fiction altogether in order to address the audience directly. Such a moment might occur during Petruchio's soliloquy at the end of Act IV, scene i. The final two lines of this speech seem to require an almost Brechtian mode of presentation, Petruchio explicitly soliciting the spectators' advice and even sympathy by suddenly shifting into what feels like a one-sided conversation (but see Samuel Taylor's and Jonathan Miller's treatment of this speech in Chapter 4). It would make for a startling moment in a modern theatrical context to follow through on the way this passage elides the division between stage and auditorium by raising the houselights briefly to allow for eye contact. In the open-air theatres of early modern England, such potential for interaction between actor and spectators was always available.

The staging of entrances and exits likewise depends on the space in which a play is performed. A proscenium arch theatre may admit of entrances only from left and right, whereas an open-air production in a park that uses a minimal set might allow a character to enter and exit from virtually any direction. The amphitheatre(s) in which this play was performed in the sixteenth century almost certainly had a stage that was accessed by three doors in the back wall: a large central doorway, and two smaller doors on either side. Theatre historians have speculated that the use of these doors, to avoid congestion and for ease of blocking, was a matter of convention – one side door, in other words, tended always to serve as the exit, the other as the entrance, with the large central opening reserved for more complicated staging (to thrust out, for example, a bed, tomb, or throne). However, an acting company, for a variety of reasons, might occasionally set aside this general rule of thumb in favour of more specialized scenic effects. In *The Shrew*, for instance, there seems at least a possibility that during the scenes set in Padua one or more stage doors might have come temporarily to represent either Tranio's lodgings or Baptista's house. In Act I, scene i, for instance, Baptista closes Bianca behind the door to his house, telling her repeatedly to '[g]o in' (l. 91, see also l. 75). Baptista's house (or rather the door to it) is then shown to the Pedant by Tranio at IV.iv.1, and this is the place to which Baptista and Tranio eventually agree not to return, deciding instead to settle the assurance at Tranio's lodgings (ll. 48–55). At the beginning of V.i, Petruchio presumably takes Vincentio to the same door (the lodgings of Tranio-as-Lucentio), indicating the direction in which the door to Baptista's house lies (ll. 7–8). The idea that Shakespeare's company might have attempted to establish in performance a correspondence between stage doors and a fictional map of Padua is tempting, but the limited evidence is inconclusive.

Modern editions of *The Shrew* are largely based on the Folio text, occasionally supplemented with the Sly passages from the text of *A Shrew*. The Folio text is not consistently marked with act and scene breaks – it opens with 'Actus primus. Scaena Prima', inserts 'Actus Quartus. Scena Prima' where we would now expect to find the start of Act IV, scene iii, and leaves the rest of the action undivided. This sort of irregularity is entirely typical both of the Folio and other early modern printed plays. Spelling in this period was not regularized, punctuation is for the most part rhetorical rather than grammatical, and passages of verse can sometimes be set as prose, and likewise prose as verse, with the result that it is difficult in places to tell which form might be intended. The punctuation, lineation and spelling of the Folio is probably not, and certainly not in every instance, Shakespearean. Such features of the text were as a matter of course subject to modification: compositors in the printing-house would relineate passages to make the text fit better on the page, and change spelling and punctuation to conform to their own personal habits.

Without claiming that the Folio presentation is particularly 'authentic' (in whatever sense one might choose to understand that word), one notes that the way passages are regularized in modern editions shapes one's impression of character, plot structure and, in some cases, theatrical delivery. In the second induction, for instance, the Folio cues the entrance of Sly's wife (the male page, Bartholomew, in disguise as a woman) with 'Enter Lady', and this actor's speeches are subsequently prompted with the speech prefix '*Lady*' or its abbreviation '*La.*'. Speech prefixes are rarely carried over into live performance, but they have a crucial impact on the reading experience, and so on the way one *imagines* a scene being played on the stage. Editors, for the sake of clarity, typically emend the wife's entry direction to 'Enter Page as a lady', and signal his/her speeches with the prefix 'Page'. These editorial modifications remind readers that Sly's 'Lady' is 'really' a boy in disguise. In effect, readers of the Folio are directed to see the *role* assumed by the onstage actor (i.e., the Lady), while readers of modern editions are directed to see the onstage *actor* playing that role (i.e., the Page).

Perhaps the greatest impact editors have on the text is in terms of suggested stagings. Stage directions in early modern drama are notoriously unreliable – exits can be overlooked, speaking characters left offstage, entrances and exits evidently misplaced, and necessary business overlooked. The Folio includes a few directions, but as the usual practice is silence, editors invent and incorporate into the text cues designed to help a reader envisage stage business. Different attitudes about playwrights' authority over staging can be found among theatre practitioners and performance studies scholars. Some argue that playwrights dictate the dialogue and, through their stage directions, at least some of the action, while others advise actors to ignore printed directions since authors control only the words spoken in performance. In the latter case, even the belief that a stage direction was written by Shakespeare need not necessarily prevent actors from staging a scene differently to suit better a particular interpretation of the action. Because there are so few stage directions in early modern print and manuscript drama, the author's control over the performance, regardless of one's position on the theoretical debate, is inevitably limited. Business suggested by an editor, on the other hand, has no special authority. Interpretation for the stage and film thus depends greatly on staging decisions taken by individual directors and companies. The 'Commentary' section (Chapter 2) distinguishes occasionally between Folio and modern editorial stage directions in order to encourage readers to imagine independently of the editor potential options and staging choices.

2 *Commentary*

INDUCTION

Induction 1

1–13 'I'll pheeze you, in faith'

The Folio introduces the play with the heading 'Actus primus. Scaena Prima' (i.e., Act I, Scene I), but editors since Rowe have described Sly's story as an 'Induction', a prelude to the main action, or framing device. Spectators obviously have no access to this sort of editorial guidance in the theatre, and so are led to assume, wrongly as it turns out, that Sly and the Hostess will remain at the heart of the plot. Directors sometimes play with this expectation by cross-casting the actors playing the Hostess and Sly as Katherina and Petruchio, and moving straight from Sly falling asleep on the ground at l. 13 to the action in Padua at I.i (see Chapter 4, pp. 138–9). The effect of this choice is to present the taming story not as a play within the play, but as Sly's dream or fantasy.

13 'Enter *a Lord* from hunting, with his train'

The entrance of a lord who speaks in verse with his huntsman about his hounds, one of which he values at the enormous price of twenty pounds, marks an abrupt shift in social status from commoners to gentry. This redirection of attention can be reinforced in performance through distinctions in costume, bearing and accent. The cue to enter as 'from hunting' is recurrent in early modern drama, and there were probably stage conventions, such as green costumes, to signal the hunt. The entry tag 'with his train' is an imprecise and open-ended direction that, like the commonplace wording 'enter as many as may be', permits staging to be responsive to resources. It is

12

possible to stage this scene with as few as two attendants who double as servingmen and huntsmen, but increasing the number of the lord's retinue of liveried servants will enhance a perception of his prestige and status.

14–69   'Sirs, I will practise on this drunken man'

The lord's sustained verbal references to servants, and to expensive and luxurious goods such as rings, wanton pictures and a silver basin full of rose-water create an impression of wealth and power. They imply that he has the resources (i.e., men and possessions to serve as actors and theatrical props) to enact convincingly Sly's supposed transformation of identity. The pretence that Sly is a gentleman is the first of many 'supposes', or layers of theatrical fiction, enacted within the play.

70–7   'Take him up gently'

This short passage is filled with intradialogic directions (directions embedded in the dialogue) for movement and sound effects: the lord commands his servant or servants to put Sly in bed, he hears the sound of trumpets, he tells a servant to go see what it heralds, and asks, perhaps of the same servant now returned to the stage, its meaning. The Folio only cues the sounding of the trumpet and the servingman's entrance; modern editors often insert into the text stage directions for the other pieces of business. The question here for performance is whether the lord's commands are necessarily obeyed. If so, when exactly are they fulfilled?

His command to 'go see what trumpet 'tis that sounds' (l. 72), for example, might be made redundant by the sudden entrance of another servant, whom he proceeds to question. Or perhaps the servant directed to 'go see' moves to the side to peer offstage while the lord speculates for two lines about the identity of the new arrival, the servant's 're-entrance' merely consisting of a turn to report his findings. Sly's exit is likewise uncertain. He might be taken off immediately, as editors often infer, or the servants might be interrupted by the sudden arrival of the players. Delaying Sly's exit could emphasize his heavy (drunken) sleep or, if he stirs, introduce a sense of sudden suspense as the other characters wonder if he will awaken; his continued presence onstage could allow the players to eye sceptically the 'lord' for whom they will act that night, or simply provide opportunity for comic business, as the lord and his men step over and around, or else try to hide, his body. Reading for performance involves attending to directions built into the dialogue, and considering how they might be shaped – or sometimes ignored – to create particular interpretative effects.

77–102   *'Enter Players'*
As with the lord's train, this direction requires substantial interpretation for performance. The play they eventually perform is the comedy of Baptista and his two daughters, and therefore one could imagine the lord welcoming as many as fifteen to twenty actors. So many unexpected visitors might add comic weight to the lord's question, 'Do you intend to stay with me tonight?', but it seems likely for reasons of expediency that only a few members of the company will enter here. Modern editions often designate the 'First Player' as the troupe's only spokesperson, but the Folio speech prefixes – '2.Player', 'Sincklo' and 'Plai[er]' – might imply a less orderly exchange in which the lord directs his comments to three individual players, each of whom replies.

'Sincklo' points outside of the narrative fiction to an actual actor in Shakespeare's company, John Sincklo, whose name, whether in cast lists or, as here, as a speech prefix, turns up in *Richard Duke of York* (*3 Henry VI*), *2 Henry IV*, and John Marston's *Malcontent*. Fittingly, this remnant of the earliest performance circumstances calls the attention of readers to the self-aware theatricality of a passage in which a fictional character instructs in the profession of acting other fictional characters playing, but also played by, professional actors.

The scene's metatheatrical energy would be further heightened if, as seems likely from the prevalence of Sincklo's name here and elsewhere, at least some of the acting troupe were comic actors already known to the spectators. A slightly different example of performance conditions breaking through the play's narrative fiction was encountered previously in the row between Sly and the Hostess. The tinker's otherwise incomprehensible reference to the Hostess as 'boy' (ll. 12) makes sense when one recalls that the women's parts were originally played by boy actors; Sly, in effect, dismisses a composite fictional/theatrical figure made up of the character of the Hostess and the actor playing her.

103–36 'see him dressed in all suits like a lady'

The lord turns from the professional players' performance to the amateur theatrics of his page, Bartholomew. The issue of a woman's duty to her husband is at the thematic heart of the play within the play, and the lord's extended lesson in how to play convincingly the woman's part offers to spectators a preliminary verbal portrayal of the constituent elements of wifely behaviour: a humble manner, quiet voice, sexual availability, and (false) tears. The lord anticipates that the humour of his practical joke will derive not from an incongruity of gender (he tells us at ll. 129–30 that the boy 'will well usurp the grace ... of a gentlewoman'), but from an incongruity of degree, which renders ludicrous the spectacle of a tinker truly coming to believe he is a lord. This framing device, insofar as it humiliates Sly's presumption in falling prey to the lord's fabricated illusion of high social status, tames the impudence of beggars and not the impudence of women.

Induction 1: Cutting the frame?

The Induction material portraying the lord's deception of Sly frames the inset play performed by the touring actors, and the two stories unfold more or less independently of one another. For such reasons as running time, casting restrictions or narrative shape, the Sly frame is often cut in performance. In these cases, the action either opens with Lucentio's entrance at Act I, scene i, or with an inserted scene such as a Punch and Judy puppet show that stands in place of Sly (see Chapter 4, p. 124). The effect of cutting the Inductions is to lose one layer of fictional distance, turning the romantic comedy with its shrew-taming action from a deliberate and self-conscious fiction, performed for the entertainment of a tinker who thinks he is a lord, into a play performed for our own amusement; without the Inductions, the audience assumes the position of Sly in relation to the inset action.

Other sets of cuts could enable the scene to drive more quickly towards the realization of the lord's practical joke yet maintain the metatheatrical distancing effect provided by Sly as an onstage audience. The lord's exchange about his dogs with the First Huntsman, for example, could be elided (ll. 14–28), as could his dismayed description of Sly asleep (ll. 32–3), along with his rehearsal of how his servants will interact with the tinker in his chamber (ll. 44–60). The effect of these particular cuts is to play down issues of social degree by providing less opportunity to develop the contrast between the lord's and Sly's relative wealth and status. The way a company shapes a script for performance is an integral part of the interpretative activity of transforming printed drama into theatrical spectacle.

Induction 2

0   *'Enter aloft Sly'*
Exactly where Sly and his attendants were situated in the early modern amphitheatres to perform this scene is uncertain (see Chapter 1, pp. 6–9). In modern performance, the staging of this scene will be responsive to a particular theatrical space and an acting company's interpretative reading of the relation of the action to its framing device. Sly and his wife might sit to one side of the stage; at the back of the stage, facing and in full view of the audience; above the stage in a balcony space; or, especially if one wants to marginalize visually the frame through which an audience watches the action of Baptista and his daughters, Sly and his wife might sit among the spectators.

1–4   **'For God's sake, a pot of small ale'**
Sly calls here and at l. 74 for 'small ale' – a weak, cheap beer produced by reusing hops a third time. His choice emphasizes distinctions of rank between his actual and assumed identity; the servants keep trying to ply him with 'sack', a more expensive imported white wine that Sly refuses as unfamiliar to him. His comment at ll. 21–2 that he has run up a tab of 'fourteen pence' with Marian Hacket for 'sheer' ale (i.e., beer and no food) suggests that he is a regular, perhaps even heavy, drinker.

The Folio entry direction refers to him not by his name but as 'the drunkard', and spectators have already seen him passed out on the stage in the first Induction. These hints lead some editors to introduce directions for Sly to receive pots of ale from his servants. However, the feigned lord could feasibly drink nothing in this scene, and much could be made in performance of his calling for, but never getting, alcohol. Stage business will determine whether an audience reads drunkenness as Sly's dominant character note and, especially if he gets and consumes his pots of ale, might serve to explain, if motivation seems desirable, his willingness in the end to adopt the fantasy that he is a nobleman.

5–15   'I am Christophero Sly'

The contrast between Sly and his surroundings is immediately emphasized through language: Sly's early speeches are prose, but he is surrounded by attendants who speak blank verse. Sly therefore seems audibly out of place in the lord's chamber. The poetic device of anaphora (two or more lines opening with verbal repetition) used by the servingmen at ll. 2–3 and again at ll. 25–6 functions to draw attention to their heightened speech, as does the lord's balanced opposition between Sly's supposed (illustrious) descent, possessions and esteem, and (foul) spirit (ll. 12–15). The turning-point in the scene, the moment Sly accepts as truth the lord's deception, is marked by his use of a set of rhetorical questions and a sudden shift from prose to verse (ll. 67–74).

16–97   'very idle words'

The reiteration of everyday names – of places such as Burton-heath and Wincot, and friends and acquaintances such as Marian and Cicely Hacket, Peter Turph and Henry Pimpernell – locates home for Sly firmly in early modern rural England. The lord and his men disrupt Sly's sense of his own relative geographical, temporal and social place by substituting for his knowledge of ordinary townsfolk and their circumstances tales of ancient and classical figures such as Semiramis, Apollo and Io. Thus the everyday and ordinary, rather than the mythical and fantastical, become the names '[w]hich never were nor no man ever saw' (l. 95). The function of names and titles as an index of social rank becomes an issue in the extended passage where Sly and his 'wife' resolve how they will address each other (ll. 102–10). The lord's manipulation of names and naming in order to disorient personal identity and establish relations of power is a strategy of control likewise adopted by Petruchio in the inset action to tame Katherina.

98–126   'Where is my wife?'

The lord's idea to dress up a boy to play a woman replicates and highlights as theatrical artifice the convention of gender role-play implicit in the players' presentation of the play within the play, as the parts of Katherina, Bianca and the Widow – like Sly's wife – were originally played by boy actors (see also the discussion of speech prefixes in Chapter 1, p. 10). However, a modern production that casts women actors in the female roles of the inset action alters drastically the metatheatrical suggestiveness of a cross-dressed male page. Instead of seeing sexual similarity among Bartholomew and the boys playing Baptista's daughters, one sees difference. This may make the layers of theatricality even more evident or, more likely, the contrast may simply render the boy's performance antiquarian, not of a piece with the women's performances.

There is no way to reproduce in modern performance the particular metatheatrical effect enabled here by the conventions of the Elizabethan stage. If all the female roles are played by boy actors, spectators will register as unusual the departure from modern theatrical conventions. If, on the other hand, the page is cast as a woman (so establishing within existing conventions sexual continuity between the female parts in the Induction and the play within the play), the same-sex frisson generated between Sly and the page when Sly tells him/her to undress and come to bed (l. 116) is lost. This is one of the moments when one realizes that modern performance, whether staged at the reconstructed Bankside Globe or in period costume, can never fully replicate the experience of Shakespeare's theatre. The performance conditions of early modern England can be reproduced on the stage but not the largely unspoken conventions that govern the ways audiences interpret that spectacle.

127–41 'It is a kind of history'

Sly's response to the lord's announcement of the players' arrival (ll. 135–6) suggests that he is unfamiliar with the term 'comedy', confusing it with the nonce-word 'comonty'. His subsequent query if the 'pleasing stuff' to which his wife refers is 'household stuff' (i.e., furniture) begins to seem like the random word associations of a drunkard. A less interventionist interpretation of the Folio, however, would read, 'Marry, I will let them play – it is not a comonty, a Christmas gambold, or a tumbling-trick?' This punctuation, albeit failing to clarify the meaning of 'comonty', suggests curiosity on the part of Sly about what exactly the players will perform, and perhaps some disappointment at the prospect of watching a play and not these other activities.

Visiting players, often masked, would arrive unexpectedly at estates during the Christmas holidays (the seasonal connection is explicit in Sly's words) to present tumbling, dances ('gambolds'), mimes and plays for the guests' entertainment. Answered with an assurance merely that the play will be 'pleasant', Sly might be understood first to pun on his wife's vague reference to 'stuff', before accepting that she will tell him nothing more than that it is a type of narrative ('history').

Is Sly engaging here in witty wordplay, or is he so far in his cups he can no longer make sense of even commonplace words such as 'comedy' and 'stuff'? No answer is available, but the danger is that one might too easily assume with the lord and his men that a tinker, who is also a drunkard, is therefore stupid. The inflection given to Sly's lines in performance (in connection with other choices, such as if and how often Sly's pot is filled with alcohol) will shape significantly different readings of his character, and add interpretative nuance to this exchange with the page.

ACT I

Act I, scene i

1–45 'I have Pisa left / And am to Padua come'

These two slightly stilted narrative speeches serve in classic fashion the function of exposition (see Chapter 1, p. 5). Spectators already familiar with the conventions of comedy might begin to anticipate that Lucentio's proposed studies will be neglected for love, particularly when Tranio enjoins his master not to devote himself to the philosophy of Aristotle (who defines virtue as the mean between two extremes) to the exclusion of Ovid (renowned for his tales of erotic desire). While Shakespeare might have handled this material more subtly in order better to disguise its functional purpose, its very awkwardness emphasizes the theatricality of the play within a play, marking a clear break between the Sly narrative and the story of Baptista and his daughters.

46–54   'Master, some show to welcome us'

The sudden entrance of the citizens of Padua complicates further the play's metatheatrical layering, creating in effect a play within a play within a play. Baptista, his daughters, and their suitors become a spectacle, or 'show' (l. 47), for Lucentio and Tranio (cued in the Folio-derived stage direction at l. 45 to 'stand by'), who in turn comprise the 'pleasing stuff' watched by Sly and his entourage, all of which action is watched by the theatre audience. This very early Shakespearean comedy stretches nearly to its limits the convention of the framing device, and tests the effect in performance of multiple and even competing windows onto a central conflict or situation. This experiment in layered perspective, handled in a technically rudimentary way here, is explored again in the 'tragical mirth' of Pyramus and Thisbe found in the more mature *Midsummer Night's Dream* and in the spying scene outside Calchas' tent staged in the even later *Troilus and Cressida*.

Pragmatic and interrelated issues prompted by this extended use of embedded narrative are stage space and realist effect. All productions are inevitably limited by the peculiarities of specific performance spaces (on staging options for this scene in the early modern theatres, see Chapter 1, pp. 7–9). However, a non-realist mode of presentation increases performance options, especially if one accepts the convention that, within the fiction of the play, a character remains undiscerned so long as other actors affect not to hear or see the actor playing that character. It is therefore not necessary for Lucentio and Tranio to hide from the others, or even for their comments at ll. 68–73 and 84 to be delivered as some form of stage whisper (as implied in some modern editions with the stage direction *'aside'*). So long as the Paduan company feign not to register Lucentio and Tranio, only the actors, and not the fictional characters they play, will hear their interjections.

55–6 'To cart her rather'

Gremio's pun, that Katherina is better suited to carting than to court-ing, alludes to early modern methods of disciplining unruly or disruptive women. Such practices tended to centre on shaming the woman by, for example, conducting her through the streets, on or behind a cart. Another particularly vicious punishment, really a form of torture, was to place a metal bridle around a woman's head, to which was attached a metal bit that fitted into her mouth. So silenced, the shrewish woman would then be 'carted' through the community, and displayed as an example to other women. Bridles were apparently set up in churches and other public places. An image of a bridled woman carved into the misericord (a supporting ledge on the underside of a hinged seat in the choir stall), still survives in Shakespeare's home town of Stratford-upon-Avon in the church in which he is buried (see Chapter 6, p. 154).

57–69 'That wench is stark mad'

Unruly relations of gender and degree are implicitly linked as forms of comic spectacle through Tranio's and the lord's choice of words: both Katherina the shrew and Sly the beggar are figured as good 'pastime' (compare Induction I.65 and I.i.68). Katherina is described by her onlookers as 'rough', a 'devil', and 'stark mad' (ll. 55, 66, 69), and violent stage business such as flinging stools around or hitting Bianca's suitors with her cap would seem to confirm her difficult, even anti-social, nature. However, the scene's prevailing discourse of disorderly female behaviour could be troubled in performance by a refusal on the part of the actor playing Katherina to conform behav-iourally to the male characters' projected image of 'shrewishness' in this, her first appearance on stage. The former interpretation would probably offer not just Tranio and Lucentio, but the theatre audience, more to look at by way of comic spectacle; the latter might seem to shift the violence to suitors who threaten to 'cart' her.

70–91 'the other's silence'

The two sisters are quickly established as foils to one another: Katherina is argumentative, Bianca is silent; Katherina challenges her father's judgement, Bianca is obedient to it; Katherina has no suitors, Bianca has many; Katherina is blamed, Bianca is praised. Bianca thus functions as a foil to Katherina since her presence, even when – especially when – silent, coupled with the constant iteration of her womanly virtue and desirability as a marriage partner, offers the ideal of femininity the other sister so utterly transgresses. This opposition between the sisters is painted in language, but the point could be reinforced visually in performance through, for instance, a costume design scheme drawing on cultural identifications of red with aggression and anger, and white – the meaning of 'bianca' in Italian – with virtue and innocence (see Chapter 4, p. 139).

92–142 'get a husband for her sister'

Baptista's sudden but steadfast resolution that Bianca shall not marry before a husband is found for Katherina seems almost tyrannous – both Gremio and Tranio describe the younger daughter as 'mewed', or walled, up in her home like a prisoner (ll. 87, 180). This development presents the obstacle that must be overcome in order to bring about a comic resolution. It also firmly establishes Baptista as a father figure who fulfils a typical blocking function by attempting to determine or otherwise control his child's choice of suitor (a type also found in *A Midsummer Night's Dream*, *Cymbeline*, *Winter's Tale* and *Merchant of Venice*). Baptista's decision thus sets in motion as early as the opening scene both the disguise and taming plots, by forcing Bianca's suitors to come at her, if at all, through deception, and encouraging them to find a prospective husband willing to marry Katherina for her money.

143–73 'I burn, I pine, I perish'

Lucentio's references to Bianca's perfumed breath and coral lips (ll. 171–2), and his metaphorical allusions, derived from Ovid and Virgil, to illicit mythological trysts (ll. 151, 165–7) are typical of the hyperbolic posturing of literary Petrarchan lovers. Lucentio sounds like a little Romeo, declaring the sufferings he is enduring for an (as yet) unrequited love in an iambic pentameter line which, despite his pain, is beautifully balanced and pointed with suitably emphatic spondaic stress (l. 152). His extravagant and self-absorbed adoration of Bianca is given a comic twist through the juxtaposition of an untouched and pragmatic Tranio who has registered, but is at first unable to convey to his lovesick master, the apparently insurmountable problem of Katherina standing in the way of any suitor attaining Bianca in marriage.

174 'Nay, then 'tis time to stir him from his trance'

This line prompts a sudden reconsideration of the play's treatment of social hierarchies. Tranio's use of the third person implies that he is speaking to himself or, more likely, to either the onstage or theatre audiences. He thus breaks the fictional illusion of the performance (that he and Lucentio are alone) in order to address the spectators, aligning himself with our more knowledgeable understanding of the action.

This metatheatrical gesture, which implicitly assumes that we, too, will consider ''tis time' to stir Lucentio – and perhaps more than time – allows the servant to transfer to and so share with the audience a recognition that his love-blinded master lacks perception, or is perhaps even dim-witted. Tranio, despite his social inferiority, takes the upper hand over Lucentio, a reversal of status that is visually reinforced later in the scene when they exchange clothes. Thus Tranio, the clever servant who manipulates circumstances and characters to serve his own purposes, comes to resemble one of the stock characters of Italian *commedia dell'arte*, a highly conventionalized form of low comedy to which Shakespeare is in this play indebted.

175–203 ''Tis hatched, and shall be so'

Decisions about how to play this short exchange in performance can shape powerfully the characterization of Lucentio. The early juxtaposition of the savvy servant and ridiculous lover might be tempered if, once startled from his revery, Lucentio conceives in the same moment as his servant the schoolmaster disguise plot, and then subsequently, and independently, plots that the servant must play the master in his absence. Alternatively, these same lines could be inflected in such a way as to imply that Lucentio, still besotted with his mistress but finally also made aware of her 'cruel' father (l. 182), mentions the provision of schoolmasters merely as evidence of Baptista's parental care, not as the early hatchings of a complex ruse. In this version, Lucentio only pretends to intuit Tranio's plot to avoid looking foolish. This gives comic emphasis both to the fast-paced series of exchanges in which the two of them refer to having come up with a plot without, however, mentioning its details (ll. 186–8), and to Tranio's eventual dismissal of 'their' plan as 'Not possible'. Lucentio's final solution, that Tranio should dress and live as a wealthy man, could be played as his predictable response to a leading question (ll. 191–4), the servant for his own purposes allowing the master to think the idea is his own.

203–17   'Uncase thee'

Sumptuary proclamations dating from the reign of Henry VIII that were in force throughout the reign of Elizabeth I and James I attempted to legislate on the basis of degree and wealth the use of certain fabrics, colours and trimming. The idea was that external appearance should always be an accurate reflection of one's actual social status, and so make impossible the sort of deception on which Lucentio's and Tranio's plotting depends: a confusion of identity among lower- and upper-ranking subjects.

The moment in which these two characters transform their positions in society simply by changing their clothes thus relies on a way of thinking about the performance of self – specifically, a presumed one-to-one relation of costume to identity – that was prevalent to the early modern imagination. The onstage costume change also, paradoxically, points to the precariousness of this system and the ironies attendant on founding a strict social hierarchy on the very costumes and props that characterize theatrical performance. The slipperiness of identity pointed to by this shape-shifting is captured by the curious coincidence that spectators wait for over two hundred lines in this scene to learn the name of Tranio's master. They finally hear 'Lucentio' three times in as many lines (ll. 213–15), just at the moment the master's name is appropriated, along with his clothes, by Tranio.

Few modern spectators not already versed in early modern

sumptuary laws will grasp, even in a period costume production, the potential ideological nuances of Tranio's and Lucentio's transforma-tions. Less rigidly codified attitudes to costume observed today in some cultures present their own design challenges to modern dress productions. In particular, in a social context in which jeans and T-shirts are worn by rich and poor, titled peer and commoner, which pieces of costume can Tranio and Lucentio exchange to signal their altered status? Modernizing this theatrical moment requires design-ers to consider the semiotics of class and privilege in the twenty-first century, and how they are read on the body.

The two actors might effect the transformation at any point between l. 199, when Lucentio first has the idea, and l. 218, when Biondello remarks on their altered appearances. An editorial stage direction, such as *'They exchange garments'*, is somewhat misleading, as it implies that the costume change happens at a particular moment. In performance it is more likely to occur over the course of several lines of dialogue, depending, in part, on decisions about whether they will exchange their outfits completely, or just swap tokens of identity, such as hats or large pieces of jewellery.

218–41 'Sirrah, where have you been?'

It seems strange to introduce not one, but two, servants, and Biondello, entering at the tail-end of a busy scene, can seem like an after-thought. However, this character serves an important func-tional purpose precisely because the other two are not proposing a straightforward reversal of identities: to pass successfully as Lucentio, Tranio needs a servant to stand in the same relationship to him as he to Lucentio. Lucentio's elaborate and transparent lie about murder and escape seems a peculiarly inept way to 'charm' some-one's tongue (l. 206), as Biondello's comic incomprehension indi-cates (l. 232). This complication is immediately forgotten (or perhaps never taken seriously in the first place), as by the fourth act Biondello is integral to the plot to secure Bianca for Lucentio.

242–5 'make one among these wooers'

This major plot development – that Tranio will not only entertain friends and keep house in Padua but also woo in Lucentio's name – is abruptly tagged onto the end of the scene. Lucentio's assurances that he has undisclosed reasons 'both good and weighty' (l. 245) smack of poorly concealed plot construction, and likely owe more to Shakespeare's art, than Lucentio's craft. Numbering Tranio among Bianca's wooers not only helps to keep Lucentio before Bianca's eyes by proxy, and introduces Baptista to the idea of a wealthy Pisan son-in-law (albeit not the man himself), but, more importantly, the device serves to frustrate the rich Gremio's strong claim to Bianca as early as the second act, when a husband for Katherina is found.

Obvious alternatives would be to invent a cause for Baptista to continue to stall in his choice of husband for Bianca, an option that might seem clumsy, or to allow Baptista and Gremio to reach an understanding and so enter Bianca into a legally binding engagement, a development which might seem awkward to resolve after the discovery in Act IV of the young lovers' elopement. The solution on which Shakespeare settles is the one provided in his source play (see Chapter 3, pp. 95–100). This disguise plot is sometimes heavily condensed and simplified for performance (see Chapter 4, pp. 120–27).

246–51 'My lord, you nod'

Is the character who accuses Sly at l. 246 of falling asleep (possibly the lord, but only identified in the Folio with the speech prefix '1 Man') a reliable commentator, or does trustworthiness rest with the tinker, who protests 'by Saint Anne' that he does indeed mark the play? Modern editorial directions that cue Sly to '*come to with a start*' adopt the former position. This is the last we hear of Christopher Sly, the page his wife, and their attendants.

The structure of Shakespeare's play has seemed incomplete to some commentators (see Chapter 1, pp. 1–4), and productions since the early twentieth century have extended the role of Sly by integrating into the action the relevant passages from *A Shrew* (reprinted in Chapter 3). However, rather than speculate about 'missing' scenes, one might see a metamorphosis of the play within a play into the play proper, a change that complements the transformations of identity that occur in the opening scene (see Chapter 6, pp. 160–1).

The main question for performance is whether Sly and the others are left onstage. The stage direction to '*sit and mark*' seems to indicate clearly that they are to remain where they are to watch the rest of the play, an interpretation reinforced by the Folio's description of them as 'Presenters' (a type of onstage chorus such as appears, for example, in Thomas Kyd's *Spanish Tragedy*). If they remain, they might be silent spectators, or a disruptive audience who heckles the actors. There is no pressing reason, however, to assume that printed directions must always be followed in performance, and these actors often slip away quietly, sometimes to return in later scenes in other roles.

Act I, scene ii

1–15   'knock me here soundly'

The opening of this scene, with the arrival to Padua of another traveller and his servant, offers a visual and verbal repetition of Lucentio's and Tranio's entry at the top of Act I, scene i. The tone and lyrical quality of Petruchio's first four lines – his blank verse apostrophe to Verona, the poetic scansion of a final syllable in 'belovèd' and 'approvèd', his choice of the verb 'trow', archaic in flavour even in Shakespeare's time – mark his speech patterns as elevated, of a piece with the type of heightened verse heard earlier from Lucentio.

The tone, however, shifts abruptly at l. 6, when Grumio responds in prose to his master's command to knock at the door. Grumio emerges as a variety of low comic character Shakespeare would favour again in such plays as *Much Ado About Nothing*, *Love's Labour's Lost*, and, in the character of the Gravedigger, *Hamlet*. He shows a tendency to malapropism, mistakenly substituting 'rebused' for 'abused' (l. 7), and to a paralysing misprision, taking 'knock' in the sense of 'to strike [someone]' rather than to rap at the door, before becoming even more muddled by interpreting as a command to strike his master, Petruchio's old-fashioned or colloquial use of the dative form 'knock [for] me' (l. 11). It remains a question for performance whether Grumio genuinely or purposefully mistakes Petruchio, but the broad comedy of this encounter depends less on any sense of the servant's potential cunning than on the master's growing exasperation and the playwright's sustained handling of an evident misapprehension.

Initial resemblances of character and situation between Petruchio and Lucentio are thus quickly eroded by comparison of their servants. Whereas Lucentio turns to Tranio for counsel and assistance almost in the manner of a friend or companion (I.i.154–5), Petruchio's comic inability to make Grumio understand a simple command to knock at the door widens, rather than minimizes, the status differential between master and servant. A potential design issue centres on how to handle these repetitions and differences in performance and, in particular, whether to point up or gloss over the disparity between the two sets of master–servant relations. For example, Grumio (especially in contrast to Tranio), could be made to seem clownish or like a bumpkin through non-verbal signals such as an ill-fitting costume, vulgar mannerisms or exaggerated accent. Such choices, however, would almost certainly flatten out potential subtleties of character by encouraging spectators to dismiss Grumio as serving 'merely' a broad comic function.

16–19   'I'll ring it'

Petruchio puns on 'ringing' a doorbell and 'wringing' Grumio's ear, implying that this (w)ringing will serve in place of knocking by sounding a musical note (i.e., Grumio's cries, figured as 'singing'). The direction for Petruchio to 'wring him by the ears' might cue histrionic pinchings that prompt loud yells without ever seriously threatening harm or, alternatively, it might be interpreted in performance as punches and blows that cause real pain. Depending on how Katherina's interaction with the suitors in Act I, scene i is staged, this might be the second time in as many scenes the audience witnesses an onstage fray. As well as finding parallels between Petruchio and Lucentio as potential suitors to Baptista's daughters, apparent similarities in temperament between Petruchio and Katherina might lead spectators to anticipate that these two might make a fit match.

Critical uncertainty about whether to read *The Taming of the Shrew* as farce or romantic comedy are relevant to this discussion of violence and its presentation on stage. The two-dimensional characterisation, low comedy and slapstick that tend to characterize farce encourage the assumption that, as in some animated cartoons, there exists a disjunction between even extreme violence and the body on which it is exerted. Violence in farce, in other words, whether physical or emotional, causes no 'real' pain or damage (see Chapter 6, pp. 152–3).

However, the usual way to tame a shrew in Elizabethan England, according to ballads and pamphlets, was precisely through the pain caused by physical cruelty (see Chapter 3, pp. 100–6). Petruchio's methods, as we eventually learn, exclude whippings and beatings, but the constant possibility of bodily violence haunts his interactions with Katherina. This moment when Petruchio's verbal threats are transformed into action – albeit taken out on a recalcitrant servant rather than an unruly wife – offers a crucial interpretative opportunity for performance. How vicious, exactly, is 'mad' Petruchio as he beats his servant? Will an audience see Grumio as seriously hurt, or do they expect him to bounce back, unmarked? Does the stage violence remain firmly within the realm of farce, or does its potential excessiveness begin to trouble generic categories?

20–35 'Alla nostra casa ben venuto'
Shakespeare frequently sets his plays in countries such as Italy, France and Bohemia, and one accepts as a convention the fact that the inhabitants of these foreign places speak English and tend to dress in the fashions of sixteenth- and seventeenth-century England (the ancient Roman tradesmen of *Julius Caesar*, most famously, throw their 'caps' in the air). The action thus often requires a sort of double vision by means of which one recognizes these places as both familiar and strange, at once set in faraway lands and in an English home. This brief exchange of pleasantries in Italian foregrounds this practice as a convention by having an uncomprehending Grumio wrongly assume that Hortensio and Petruchio are speaking Latin, a language of the educated. The joke, available presumably only to an educated élite (and Italians), is on Grumio, this most English of Italian servants, and on a bemused audience, caught out by Shakespeare's metatheatrical play.

36–46 'Petruchio, patience'
Curiously, and as the argument threatens to break out once again, Hortensio intervenes in a moot case to check Petruchio's anger, not Grumio's insolence. Even more significantly, Hortensio's assumption

of the function of arbitrating mediator has the effect of making both sides of the fray look and sound like squabbling children. Petruchio's entrance into the action of the play is humorous, but he catches our attention precisely because he is comically ineffectual and impotent, unable to control his own servant even through the threat (and execution) of physical violence. Hortensio's generous description of Grumio at l. 46, easily rendered ironic in performance, may suggest that Grumio is particularly difficult to get along with, but, notably, the pattern of behaviour between master and servant seems well established. This raucous episode hardly offers the introduction one might expect to a character who will emerge in the final scene a celebrated shrew-tamer, and it perhaps lays an early seed of doubt whether Petruchio will, indeed, be able to break Katherina's will to his own.

47–55   'Antonio, my father, is deceased'

This is one of the first things spectators learn about Petruchio, and he repeats it in this scene three times. How the news of Antonio's death is delivered by Petruchio and received by his auditors will shape to various effect an early impression of the future wife-tamer. Often the repetition is put to purely comic effect. Miller, for example, had the actors playing Petruchio and Grumio three times and with the same gestures seem to brush away condolences. But a perception that Petruchio genuinely mourns the loss of his father, an effect generated in Monette's production, can soften his characterization as a wife-tamer, making him seem capable of genuine affection (see Chapter 4). Marowitz, by contrast, used the moment to emphasize Petruchio's brutality by having the actor only seem to mourn Antonio's death before bursting out in laughter and so discomfiting Baptista.

56–128   'I come to wive it wealthily in Padua'

In this unexpected encounter with an old friend, Hortensio finds in Petruchio the man 'so very a fool' (I.i.123) to marry a rich, but troublesome, woman. The effect of their extended exchange about suitable marriage partners is to inflate the notoriety of the absent Katherina, transforming her in our (and Petruchio's) mind's eye from Baptista's eldest daughter into a figure of nearly mythological

proportions through such devices as evasion (ll. 62–3), classical allusion and amplification (ll. 68–73), hyperbole (ll. 76–81) and simile (ll.
94–5), Hortensio's description culminating with the alliterative
soubriquet, 'of all titles the worst': Katherine the curst (l. 126). This
woman, already metaphorically likened to an animal (a shrew), thus
comes to seem through comic exaggeration a fearful monster, and
Petruchio the combatant prepared to tackle her in marriage, thereby
freeing from her tyranny and her tongue both the imprisoned Bianca
and the local townsmen.

This view of Petruchio as heroic saviour is qualified by the
constant reiteration of Katherina's wealth: his ruthless opportunism
is directly proportional to her monstrosity. Whereas Hortensio
metaphorically figures the beautiful Bianca as the 'treasure' and
'jewel' he seeks (ll. 116–18), and flatly states that neither poverty on his
side nor 'a mine of gold' on hers would entice him to marry her sister
(ll. 90–1), Petruchio's ambitions are crudely literal: the only quality he
values in a bride is a rich dowry. His single-minded willingness to
'board' the shrew (ll. 94–5) is an obvious plot device necessary to
release Bianca and so develop the romantic comedy, and it further
creates an expectation of even more farcical spectacle and noise to
come.

Crucially, though, his preoccupation with money could equally
imply that he is a social climber, aligning him with – and leaving him
vulnerable to the same ridicule as – the transgressive Sly, a jumped-
up beggar dressed as a nobleman (see Chapter 6, p. 155). An audience's perception of Petruchio's personal wealth thus becomes a key
interpretative issue. If his costume and bearing portray him as a
substantial nobleman of means, issues of status are less relevant to a
spectator's assessment of motivation; if, however, his costume is
threadbare, or stage business is devised to imply that the 'crowns in
[his] purse' and 'goods at home' are few, the visitor from Verona
could potentially seem as transgressive of orderly societal hierarchies
as his prospective wife.

129–40 'Here's no knavery!'

Grumio's editorial interjection (ll. 136–7) not only speaks to
Hortensio and his plot to evade Baptista's determination to bar from

his home suitors for Bianca, but also Lucentio, who is attempting the same deception and enters at this moment in disguise as the Latin tutor, Cambio. Grumio comes to function in this scene as a sort of satiric prose chorus. In particular, he embellishes and amplifies Petruchio's conviction to marry a rich woman at any price.

At ll. 109–14, Grumio introduces an obscure pun concerning 'a figure' that will 'disfigure' Katherina. This wordplay is often interpreted as an extended conceit on 'railing', Grumio warning that Katherina's scolding is no match for Petruchio's verbal 'rope-tricks' ('figure' thus meaning 'figure of speech'). However, the violence of this speech, and of a set of connecting images that constructs rhetoric as a sort of metaphorical acid thrown in an opponent's face is reminiscent of the physical violence witnessed at the beginning of the scene. Grumio's prediction about how a wrangle between Petruchio and Katherina will conclude thus keeps before one's eyes the spectre of the familiar shrew-taming violence.

141–60   'A proper stripling and an amorous!'

The Folio calls Gremio a 'pantaloon' in his first entry direction (I.i.45), a description that immediately establishes for readers that he is akin to a stock character of *commedia dell'arte* – the rich, miserly old merchant who is always duped, often by a beautiful young woman who cuckolds him. Grumio's ironic reaction as Gremio enters coaching Lucentio how to woo Bianca on his behalf (l. 141), along with his later descriptions of him as a 'woodcock' and an 'ass' (l. 158), would seem to confirm the characterization.

The assumption that the pantaloon will not win the woman or, if he manages to wed her, will not satisfy her sexually, grows out of deep-seated cultural prejudices against age disparities in marriage. That said, Gremio remains a serious obstacle to the other suitors precisely because he is rich and, tellingly, he is the only one, other than the false Lucentio, to enter into negotiations with her father in Act II, scene i. Grumio's comments on this character at lines 158 and 175 thus encourage an audience to share a conventionalized view of Gremio as rich, ridiculous and gullible.

Performance, however, might subvert this interpretation, at least temporarily, to open up very different dynamics among the suitors. For instance, if one sets aside the description of Gremio as a 'pantaloon', there is no reason why Grumio's spontaneous reaction to Gremio as a 'proper [i.e., handsome] stripling' should be played entirely for irony. The perception that Gremio is a serious, rather than faintly ludicrous, contender in the play's marriage stakes might be further supported if the actor playing this character is cast and costumed against type, perhaps as a well-groomed entrepreneur advanced in years, handsome and sophisticated. Considering where and how performance might depart from conventional attitudes to even stock characterization can make available otherwise unexplored avenues of interpretation.

161–215 'Tush, tush, fear boys with bugs!'

Three times, and from three different angles, Gremio checks that Petruchio knows what he is getting into, keeping the enormity of the task constantly before his, and the audience's, eyes (ll. 184–94). His disbelief eventually prompts Petruchio to set out his credentials in eloquent and poetically heightened blank verse, in effect offering his sceptics the *curriculum vitae* of a would-be shrew-tamer. A noisy homelife, as Gremio and Hortensio indicate, is the penalty for marrying a turbulent woman. Petruchio dismisses this trouble as insignificant by describing in turn the fearful things he has heard in the natural world and on the battlefield, summoning up the power of these sounds with a series of balanced, rhythmically repetitive, and emphatically pointed rhetorical questions that strike the ears of his auditors like blows. A woman's tongue, by comparison, is likened to a chestnut bursting in the fire.

The sense of comic deflation prompted by his sudden oratorical shift from the public to domestic space is reinforced by a corresponding metrical shift at line 205 to the relative lyricism of regular iambic pentameter. Petruchio's confidence, conveyed through the substance and form of this *tour de force* speech, transforms Katherina's noise from a source of real fear to the imagined sprites used to frighten children, and satisfies his onstage audience once and for all that he is the man for the job. Whether the theatre audience believes that the refrain 'Have I not . . .' should necessarily be answered in the affirmative – that his rhetoric, in other words, is anything more than bluster – is another matter.

216–47 'Well begun, Tranio.'

Lucentio's entrance earlier in this scene as the tutor, Cambio, drew attention less to his disguise than to the dramatic irony of Gremio offering to one of his rivals painstaking instructions on how to sue for Bianca's love with perfumed letters, fair words and erotic stories from Ovid. Potential apprehension about how well he will perform in this assumed role is diminished as he comes on already secure in his new identity, in the company of a gulled Gremio. In Tranio's case, however, spectators watch him walk on stage in disguise as a nobleman and encounter for the first time a large group of men, some or all of whom are themselves wealthy and noble. The interest, even suspense, that this entrance inspires is generated precisely by our knowledge that he is an impostor: there seems at least the possibility that he may not 'pass' as a crossdresser.

Tranio's performance depends not only on his 'brave' costume (l. 215), but on assuming the language of his social superiors – significantly, then, he immediately adopts with these strangers an aggressive posture. Gremio, Petruchio and Hortensio each refuses to answer his request for directions to Baptista's house. Tranio subtly reverses the power dynamics first by declining to answer their questions, then by threatening to exit, so forcing them within ten lines to sue to him for information (ll. 225–6). Only when Gremio and Hortensio turn on each other does he finally present himself as a third suitor to Bianca in an elegantly worded speech that carefully avoids seeming to ask their leave.

Each of these male characters postures and jockeys to assert his authority over the others, and Tranio's success in his assumed part is signalled by his ability to shoulder his way into this homosocial dynamic. Gremio and Petruchio both comment on his strange language (ll. 245, 247), a sign that he stands apart from them and so perhaps is not yet entirely proficient with his new role, but the performance is good enough to gain him access as a nobleman to Paduan society. How good his performance seems to the theatre audience, however, will depend as much on voice, gesture and bearing as on the actual words he speaks. In Jonathan Miller's production, for example, Tranio's accent gives him away to the audience, but not within the fiction of the play, as an imposter (see Chapter 4, p. 133).

Gremio, Hortensio, Lucentio and Tranio are notoriously difficult to keep straight when reading the text, particularly once they start shifting in and out of complicated disguise intrigues. However, the actors' bodies and costuming choices in performance help spectators to distinguish the characters, and shape a sense of their relative suitability for marriage. This scene, which assembles on stage at one time all of the suitors to Baptista's daughters, encourages spectators to appraise each character by measuring how he differs from the other characters. Casting decisions made before rehearsals begin can thus have an immense impact on how an audience responds to the action. One might expect Lucentio, for example, the suitor who eventually wins Bianca's heart and hand, to be played by a young, handsome actor. How, then, might the sexual dynamics of the comedy shift if the actor most easily recognized as the 'leading man' type is cast as Tranio, not Lucentio? How does Petruchio's age compare to that of Lucentio and Gremio? Does Petruchio seem more, or less, of a catch than Lucentio? And how might each of these casting details confirm or disrupt in the closing scene a perception of comic resolution?

248–79   'well you do conceive'

Hortensio and Gremio have bribed Petruchio to marry Katherina, not only promising that Baptista will provide a rich dowry but agreeing to cover all of his expenses in courtship if he is successful in his suit (ll. 180–83). Homosocial competition and money are the coordinates that determine the men's interactions with each other, and Tranio sustains his authority within this network of relations by intuiting and anticipating their arrangement, offering, unprompted, to recompense Petruchio's efforts (ll. 262–7). His status was further elevated in Monette's production at the end of the scene when he proposed drinking toasts to their mistresses' health while ostentatiously displaying his American Express card (see Chapter 4). The bribe, glancingly touched on in this scene and never mentioned again, provides the context for a major turning point in the relationship between Kat (Katherina) and Verona (Petruchio) in the high school comedy *10 Things I Hate about You*.

ACT II

Act II, scene i

1–30   'Unbind my hands'

The construction of early modern drama is guided by the convention that a character who exits one scene will not immediately re-enter the following scene (exceptions can be cited, but they are remarkable because rare). This dramaturgical rule of thumb explains, in part, the introduction here of a little vignette between Katherina and Bianca: seven characters exit the stage at the end of Act I, leaving potentially available for the beginning of the following scene only Baptista and his daughters.

In addition to accommodating the pragmatic restrictions of writing for the early modern stage, the women's argument transfers the action from a public to domestic space, and develops the characterization of the daughters. The control at first seems to rest entirely with Katherina as Bianca, her hands tied as though to reproduce visually her suitors' metaphorical image of her as the prisoner of her sister (I.i.87–9, I.ii.115–23), tries to second-guess what she has that her sister might envy. She offers to give her 'gauds' (or, as printed in the Folio, 'goods'), her clothes, and either of her two suitors, Hortensio and Gremio. But Bianca's generosity (or desperation) makes tangible everything she has that Katherina might envy while making it explicit that she thinks Katherina has cause to envy her. The power of the younger sister to provide what she presumes the other lacks reverses the dynamics, but makes the match between them no more even.

This passage is filled with staging that is implicit in the dialogue: Bianca's repeated request to Katherine to 'unbind/untie my hands' (ll. 4, 21) suggests her hands are bound; Baptista's pity for his youngest daughter implies he finally frees her; his command to 'stand aside' (l. 24) might prompt a movement; and his observation that 'she weeps' (l. 24) seems to signal that the actor playing Bianca should by that point be in tears. Performance, however, will always exceed the spoken (and printed) word. For instance, assuming a production follows the intradialogic direction to have Bianca enter with her hands tied, precisely how they are tied will inflect an audience's response in a particular way: is she led on by a rope held by her sister? Is she tied to something? Is she also blindfolded? Alternatively, Baptista might 'see' non-existent tears in his daughter's eyes, or his assumption that 'she weeps' might prompt the pretense of crying from a manipulative Bianca.

Actors, moreover, can invent, as well as find in the dialogue, opportunities for perhaps unexpected stage business. What prompts, for example, Katherina's accusation, 'Her silence flouts me', and the Folio-derived direction *'She flies after Bianca'*? Perhaps no incentive is necessary, especially if one accepts Baptista's blunt estimation of Katherina as a 'hilding of a devilish spirit' (l. 26). However, productions in which Bianca grimaces or sticks out her tongue at her sister out of Baptista's line of sight reshape entirely our attitude to Katherina and her family. Shakespeare provides in his dialogue instructions for performance, but in a particular production some of them will be ignored, others reimagined, and much other stage business, impossible to encode in a printed text, simply invented.

31–7 'She is your treasure'

Katherina's accusation that Baptista favours his younger daughter, especially when set alongside his promise to Bianca at I.i.76–101 of his continued love and attention, has led some critics to argue that parental cruelty or neglect is the cause of Katherina's disruptive and attention-seeking behaviour (see Chapter 4, pp. 134–6 for Baptista's favouritism and Katherina's corresponding resentment as handled in Miller's production). Petruchio's tough love might in this way be distanced from the physical and ideological brutality of shrew-taming, and presented as the means by which Katherina is empowered to escape both her family and the self-destructive defensive mechanisms on which she has come to depend.

38–60 'His name is Licio.'

The feasibility of Lucentio's and Tranio's disguise plot ostensibly rests on their recent arrival to Padua, and the fact that nobody can yet distinguish their faces (I.i.196–8). Such concerns, more typical of realist drama, are just as easily dispensed with in early modern drama, as this scene reveals. Bianca has previously had two rivals in love, Gremio and Hortensio, both of whom are well known to the family and each other. Hortensio decides to gain access to Baptista's home in disguise as Licio, the music teacher, and suddenly becomes unrecognizable to his neighbours – not even his inexplicable absence from the side of his competitor, Gremio, prompts the others to see Hortensio in Licio.

The convention of disguise, well evidenced by crossdressed gender comedies such as *As You Like It* and *Twelfth Night*, is that not even close family members can see through the most rudimentary costume change. Whereas in Tranio's case part of the energy of his roleplay derives from his transgression of the boundaries of degree and the seemingly real possibility that the supposed Lucentio might be scandalously exposed as a servant, the very unlikelihood that Hortensio could pass as a servant among his neighbours releases a production from any need for realist disguise. His costume might be as convincing as a complete physical make-over will allow, as basic as a change of clothes, or even deliberately farcical (an obviously fake wig and beard, silly glasses, loud trousers). Choosing among this range of possibilities depends on determining how, precisely, a production wants to shape spectators' expectations of this character – farcical costuming, for example, would probably add humour to Hortensio's re-entry later in the scene, 'his head broke' by Katherina, but would also almost inevitably develop this character as a fool and so never a serious contender for Bianca's hand.

61–101   'Let us . . . speak too'

Each suitor offers courteous language and gifts of tutors or materials of instruction to try to set himself most in Baptista's favour. The spirit of competition reappears, even between men who are not rivals for the same woman, with Gremio taking offence at Petruchio's presumption as a newcomer to advance himself and his gift without giving priority, as it were, to the resident suitor. Whether Gremio's sharpness is just a belated effort to reassert his own priority, or whether Petruchio indeed seems 'marvellous forward' (l. 73), disrespectful of 'orderly' form (l. 45), and so, perhaps, of Baptista, will depend largely on performance and the father's choice of non-verbal signals.

In particular, the moment of his rejection of Petruchio's suit (ll. 61–6) is ambiguous: it might be lightly glossed over, or else delivered in such a way as to suggest that his 'grief' is not that his daughter is unsuitable for Petruchio, but that Petruchio is unsuitable for her. How this exchange between father and potential suitor is played will inform both a sense of Petruchio's character and, especially if the latter option is played, the price Baptista is willing to pay later in the scene to marry off his eldest daughter (see Chapter 4).

Verse is commonly reserved in Shakespeare's drama for characters of elevated rank, while prose is the form usually spoken by servants and commoners. However, the shifts between verse and prose in *The Taming of the Shrew* are remarkably fluid, and it is sometimes difficult to tell which is being used. Tranio's and Lucentio's exit lines at I.i.236–45 are printed in the Folio as a combination of prose and verse (the servant speaks prose, the master verse), but the whole passage might well be either prose or doggerel verse. In Act II, scene i, by contrast, we hear Gremio rebuke Petruchio's bluntness in verse before he shifts to a more familiar, yet still heightened, prose to present to Baptista Cambio's services as a Latin tutor. Baptista accepts, likewise graciously, in prose. Tranio, as though to insist on his (pretended) high rank, avoids replying to Baptista in prose, shifting back to verse. It remains a question how readily audible this complex interplay of verse and prose would seem in performance.

102–10 'Lucentio is your name?'

Tranio has yet to introduce himself to Bianca's father, and so unless one devises physical business by which one can resolve in performance how Baptista comes up with his name, there is an apparent glitch in the plot. Editors often introduce a stage direction cueing Baptista to open one of the books to find Lucentio's name on the fly-leaf. This business was used in Jonathan Miller's BBC/Time-Life production; to very different effect, Richard Monette's Stratford, Ontario production had Tranio as Lucentio present to Baptista his calling card. Quite apart from the fact that spectators are unlikely to notice, or care about, a minor inconsistency in a busy scene, the action's sustained metatheatricality – the constant emphasis through such devices as disguise and inset narratives that this is 'just' a play – discourages too careful an attention to realist circumstances. Such business is feasible, but not essential.

III–29   'my business asketh haste'

Petruchio brushes aside the niceties of courtship to focus on money, a concern that, at least among wealthy or noble early modern families, remained at the heart of marriage negotiations. The jointure he promises to settle on Katherina – a contractual agreement by means of which his wife will be provided for financially after his death – is property: his lands and their rental value. Katherina's dowry – what her father contractually obliges himself to provide on the occasion of his daughter's marriage – is half his lands after he dies, and 20,000 crowns (5000 pounds) on the wedding day.

A proclamation regulating London wages which dates from 1587, about five years before the first performance of *The Taming of the Shrew*, provides some idea of the immense value of this dowry in real money: in addition to food and drink the best shoemakers, tailors and hosiers could expect to earn £4 in a year, the best clothworkers £5, and the best alebrewers, blacksmiths, butchers and cooks £6. To the groundlings who spent one penny to stand in the pit to watch a play in early 1590s London, 20,000 crowns would seem an astronomical sum of money. Extra-textual business could be devised to nuance these cut-and-dry business negotiations. Petruchio, for example, might hear the offer of land at line 121 and, with a long pause and sceptical look, make it comically clear that Baptista needs to sweeten the deal before his eldest daughter can be married off – so prompting the huge money gift.

Baptista, one should note, never firmly establishes, here or elsewhere, the monetary value of Petruchio's offer, apparently taking on trust his claim that he has 'bettered rather than decreased' (l. 118) the wealth left to him by his father. Again, this is the sort of loose end, alongside Petruchio's evident desire for ready cash, that a production could develop, suggesting comically – or even tragically – that Baptista pays a stranger to rid him of his daughter.

130–46   *'Enter Hortensio'*

Petruchio develops a sequence of metaphors from nature to characterize the necessary outcome of any combat between Katherina's pride and his own authority. The timing of Hortensio's entrance, wounded, comically punctures Petruchio's words, if not his confidence (although in performance the effect might rather be 'and' his confidence), by seeming to provide Katherina's silent answer (see Chapter 4).

147–68 'she hath broke the lute to me'

Baptista, the straight man, feeds lines to the tutor which are easily played on to comic effect. Hortensio first offers the incongruous comic juxtaposition of the soldier's and musician's professions through a turn at l. 145 on 'prove' (with a secondary pun on the verb to mean 'test' as well as 'show herself to be'), before punning on 'break' (l. 148) to mean both 'train' and 'render in pieces'. These initial sallies build to a spirited account of Katherina's music lesson.

The advantage of relating this encounter through the distancing strategy of a storytelling device rather than by presenting it first-hand on stage is that it complicates immensely the layers of perspective. The theatre audience simultaneously registers the slapstick action of Katherina smashing the lute over her tutor's head, the tutor's commentary on the action (with the vivid comparison at l. 156 of his head in the lute to one standing in the stocks), and the effect of the tutor's narration on his onstage audience. Bringing Hortensio onstage with the broken lute still on his head would replicate visually the image summoned up by his words. The function of this episode within the play's larger structure is to delay Petruchio's first introduction to Katherina and, by means of this delay, both to make the outcome of their contest seem less certain than Petruchio would suggest, and to make an audience anticipate even more eagerly their impending meeting.

168–81 'Say that she frown'

Petruchio's strategy is to counter Katherina's reported obstreperousness with a form of 'weak' strength. Instead of employing language as a means to communicate – and so, on report of Katherina's past behaviour, to transform it into a weapon of anger and conflict, ultimately prompting physical violence and a total breakdown of relations – Petruchio plans to use language as a weapon of *mis*communication, disempowering from the outset her ability to communicate at all. Everything she says that is hostile in tone or content he will take in its contrary sense. This tactic is foreshadowed at lines 42–53 and 160–2 by his paradoxical description of her as 'bashful' and 'mild'.

Petruchio might thus be interpreted as learning – like Lucentio – from his servant. In his earliest moments on stage he was utterly at a loss in face of Grumio's inability, or flat refusal, to understand his plain meaning. In terms of language, then, he simply decides to play Grumio to Katherina's Petruchio. This speech might be delivered in performance nervously or with confidence, either suggesting that Petruchio has known all along how to deal with Katherina, or that he is thinking on his feet, making it up as he goes along.

182–94 'my super-dainty Kate'

The name 'Kate' has been heard just twice previously, and always within a family context – Bianca uses it at the beginning of this scene (2.1) and Baptista also uses it just before sending his daughter to her suitor. Petruchio thus assumes a familiarity that Katherina immediately challenges. If the actor playing Katherina makes as though immediately to exit the stage, dismissing a suitor who fails even to get her name right, the flamboyancy and daring of a speech in which Petruchio repeats eleven times in six lines (185–90) the rejected version of her name could be used as a way once again to attract her attention and prevent her from leaving.

Rather than defer to her implicit rebuke, and so seem intimidated by Katherina's arch manner, Petruchio uses repetition, alliteration, amplification and heavy metrical emphasis ironically to elevate the diminutive form of her name to the stature of a title – 'Kate of Kate Hall', 'Kate of my consolation' – thereby mocking as equally inappropriate and self-important her rejoinder to his greeting. The complex wordplay on 'dainty' to mean, as a noun, a choice delicacy or 'cate', and as an adjective, both valuable and (overly) scrupulous about details, is likewise slippery, as Petruchio at once praises her worth and ridicules her imperious behaviour. This early clash about names and naming foreshadows the sun–moon scene (Act IV, scene v) and the peculiar way Petruchio displays there his absolute linguistic power within marriage.

195–235 'my tongue in your tail?'
This extended passage of stichomythia (a rapid and highly stylized verbal exchange in which a one- or two-line, even half-line, speech from one character is balanced and so exactly countered by a riposte from his or her opponent) creates an effect of emotional intensity and intimacy at the very moment the characters are engaged in a combat of words. This competitive style of dialogue, a type of verbal tennis, reproduces the physicality and muscular energy of improvized performance as spectators mark how each rejoinder becomes in turn the raw material out of which the next rejoinder is constructed. The excitement of this style of writing in performance results not just from a virtuoso display of fast-paced wordplay and bawdy innuendo, but from an anticipation that at some point the repartee will collapse, one or other of the speakers, as it were, dropping the ball.

This crucial moment occurs at line 216, with Petruchio topping Katherina's parting shot with an oral sex pun on tale/tail. Katherina's failure to reply – perhaps shocked into silence, helpless with laughter, or cut off by an opponent who shifts into a slower-paced mode – especially when coupled with a slap, means that she loses the contest. Curiously, it is Katherina who, rather than taking the opportunity at line 218 to exit as promised, sparks off once again the verbal jousting, punning on 'cuff' as an article of clothing (in Shakespeare's England, a lace accessory to a sleeve) and 'arms' in the heraldic sense of 'coat of arms' (ll. 219–21). The motivation for this decision is unclear, and might be played in performance as continued hostility and defiance, recognition that in hitting Petruchio she has overstepped the rules of the game, or a sudden understanding that when Petruchio threatens to 'cuff' her in retaliation she is indeed in potential physical danger (see Chapter 4, pp. 133–4).

The second time the repartee breaks down is at line 233. Petruchio's riposte remains incomplete perhaps because, as some editors suggest, Katherina 'struggles' in Petruchio's arms. However, it seems equally likely that it is Petruchio who finds himself struggling, unable to find the next volley of words. His reference to Katherina's 'scape' would not, then, allude to her physical resistance, but to his unwillingness to concede defeat. The staging of this important first meeting can only be (provisionally) decided in performance, whether that is on stage or in one's imagination, but the scene's unspoken physical business – the actors' proximity, and how often and in what manner they touch each other – will shape an audience's perception of the shifting power relations between the characters.

236–73 'I will marry you'

Petruchio finally employs the strategy of perverse contradiction promised in his soliloquy, claiming that he finds Katherina 'passing gentle'. His flattery, however, is edged. By itemizing the ways in which he finds 'report a very liar' Petruchio rhetorically isolates Katherina as someone who fails to fit in. His extended comparison of her (slanderously reported) limp to the 'princely gait' of the goddess of chastity, often motivated in performance by loss of a shoe, or an injury sustained during their verbal battle, likewise hides a sting. His elegantly balanced opposition of Kate in her chamber to Diana in her grove concludes with the implicit antithesis of a 'chaste' goddess and 'sportful', or sexually promiscuous, Kate. This slight touches off yet another verbal sparring match, abruptly cut short, however, when Petruchio announces in 'plain terms' that, like it or not, her father has agreed to their marriage.

Polemical tracts in late sixteenth-century Protestant England emphasized the importance of compatibility and even love between a husband and wife. Conduct book literature such as the anonymous *Tell Trothes New Yeares Gift* denounced constrained marriages as against God's word and the holy state of matrimony, especially where the marriage contract functioned, in effect, as a business deal between families seeking either to advance or attain wealth and/or social standing. Sermons likewise preached that a wife is a man's 'yoke-fellow' and helper (see Chapter 3, pp. 114–16). However, children from wealthy and/or noble families, in particular, remained on the whole severely restricted in their choice of life partner: whether or not the bride and groom were well-matched might be a factor, but would rarely be the only consideration. Baptista insists that Katherina's love is 'all in all' (l. 129), but Petruchio assumes – correctly, as it proves – that where there is such a huge financial stake (Baptista, after all, stands to gain great wealth and powerful connections through Bianca's marriage), money, and only money, will prevail with her father. Read from the perspective of early modern social history, the promise that Petruchio is the man to 'tame' her – the first time this verb appears in the play – alongside the news that her dowry has been agreed, is ominous. He no longer seems the 'movable' (l. 197) Katherina had initially assumed.

274–317 'I'll see thee hanged'

Petruchio's achievement in this passage is to gain from Baptista and the men who enter with him tacit permission to impose his own meaning on Katherina's language, so transforming 'I'll see thee hanged on Sunday first' into a statement of eager compliance. The challenge for any modern production is to devise business able to explain why, after flatly rejecting his projected date of marriage, the previously articulate Katherina suddenly falls silent. Does she signal through movement and gesture that for some reason she now accepts his offer? Is she too shocked to speak? Has she been incapacitated, perhaps through a gag or excessive consumption of alcohol? Or should one simply accept that here, as at other key moments, realist effect on the Shakespearean stage is not always a priority? David Garrick bridged this silence by adding lines for Katherina, and so motivation; Taylor had Baptista and Petruchio simply ignore her objections, but a long kiss at the line 'And kiss me, Kate' that she at first resists but to which she eventually surrenders suggests in Taylor's film that Katherina finds Petruchio sexually attractive (see Chapter 4, p. 127).

Her shared Folio exit with Petruchio at line 317, difficult to justify either in terms of psychological motivation or plot development (Petruchio has just bid her farewell), is a pragmatic piece of stagecraft removing any further opportunity for her to speak. A Shrew finds an explanation for Katherina's silence by introducing a three-line aside: 'But yet I will consent and marry him, / For I methinks have lived too long a maid, / And match him, too, or else his manhood's good'.

318–24 'now I play a merchant's part'

Baptista's two-line commentary on the sudden betrothal of Katherina makes explicit his uncertainties about Petruchio's suit, as

he figures himself – using a metaphor that draws out his own financial interest in his daughters' marriages – as a merchant undertaking
a high-risk enterprise. What the image leaves unresolved, however, is
whether his concerns are commercial, implying either that a familial
connection to Petruchio might prove down the line to be poor business or that there is a chance yet that his goods (Katherina) might
return to him unsold, or personal, his reservations stemming from a
dim view of their future emotional happiness and well-being as a
couple – or both. Tranio's business-like response, that women as
commodities have a sell-by date and so Baptista might as well risk a
bad venture as not shift her at all, continues Baptista's metaphor of
marriage as a market.

The physical details of the actors' delivery of these lines – whether
they slap each other on the shoulder, burst out laughing, or stand
quietly apart from one another – will inform how an audience interprets what they have just seen. Rhyming couplets (two iambic
pentameter lines marked with end-rhymes) are frequently used in
early modern drama to signal the end of a scene (see, for instance,
I.ii.278–9 and III.ii.89–90), and the introduction of one at lines 316–17
lends a mid-scene flourish to Petruchio's and Katherina's exit, marking this for them as the end of the scene. The slightly unusual use of
rhyming couplets at lines 319–20 and 323–4 likewise marks a strong
sense of closure, prompting a clear shift from one plot thread to the
next.

325–84 'what can you assure her?'

The relation between marriage and markets continues as a central
theme. Katherina's dowry and jointure have been settled, and now
Baptista negotiates the financial terms according to which a husband is
chosen for Bianca. What an audience sees, in effect, is repetition with a
difference: Katherina goes to the only buyer, while Bianca goes to the
wealthiest. The value at which Baptista's youngest daughter is priced is
drawn out – potentially comically so – by Gremio's careful and elaborately detailed audit of his treasure, goods, cattle and land holdings,
which is then followed up by an inflated (and, at least in Tranio's case,
in large part financially unsupported) bidding war into which the two
suitors enter. Remarkably, particularly in contrast to the opening of

this scene, no explicit mention is made of a dowry for Bianca. The implication is either that she is her own dowry, or that a competitive number of suitors has rendered the dowry non-negotiable.

Having a disguised Tranio bargain for Bianca in his master's place distances Lucentio from the business aspects of marriage and so sustains the illusion – in sharp distinction to the effect created by Petruchio's hands-on involvement in the matter of Katherina's dowry – that Bianca and her successful suitor marry for romantic love rather than out of self-interested financial profit. On the contrary, however, Vincentio's passing comment that he will 'content' Baptista (V.i.123) implies that the negotiations undertaken by a sham son in Act II, scene i and confirmed by a sham father in Act IV, scene iv, are made good by the true son and father after the marriage (see Chapter 3, p. 108 for the father's very different reaction to his son's elopement in *A Shrew*). A production that chose to cut lines 339–52, 358–63 and 365–78 for reasons of pace, running time, or even because of the obscurity of some of the language would create a scene that seemed less like an auction, and therefore perhaps make Petruchio seem an even harder-nosed opportunist.

385–404   'supposed Lucentio / Must get a father'

A first-born son inherited his wealth and title upon his father's death, having nothing with which to support himself in the meantime apart from an allowance, should his father give him one (note Vincentio's outrage at V.i.60–1 when he complains that he 'play[s] the good husband at home' while his son and servant 'spend all at the university'). This in part explains the importance of the information that Petruchio's father has recently died (I.ii.53, 101, 189). Unlike Lucentio, Petruchio's means, such as one assumes they are, are possessed, not promised. Baptista's insistence that Tranio-as-Lucentio must assure the money by getting his father to sign over his assets to his son *before* he dies thus presents a problem.

Tranio's solution, framed in terms of the paradox of a son begetting a father, makes even more complex the disguise plot, and implies the possibility of increased farcical confusion. The use of soliloquy to work through the problem, rather than, say, by means of a dialogue with Biondello, enhances an audience's sense of connectedness to

Tranio, an effect otherwise granted in this play primarily to Petruchio. The repetition at lines 400–1 of 'supposed' (meaning 'feigned' or 'counterfeit') is a verbal allusion to Gascoigne's *Supposes*, one of Shakespeare's source materials (see Chapter 3, pp. 95–100).

ACT III

Act III, scene i

1–15 'you grow too forward'

This short scene is Shakespeare's own invention (see Chapter 1, p. 6 for a discussion of its treatment of fictional location in relation to the early modern stage). In effect, it embraces three scenes in one, with Lucentio's and Hortensio's suits of love staged as separate inset dramas within the fiction of Bianca's music and Latin lessons. The scene offers a structural counterpoint to Katherina's earlier encounter with Petruchio: where the elder sister has one suitor to whose will she is subjected, Bianca has two suitors over whom she exerts both her will and power of choice. Katherina and Petruchio, alone on stage, are brought into close verbal – even in some productions sustained physical – contact through their highly charged sparring match. Bianca's suitors, by contrast, contending simultaneously with the competing distractions of a potential mistress and a potential rival, shift uneasily between protesting their love and protecting their claim.

The farcical energy of this scene, each suitor/tutor attempting to keep surveillance over the other while at the same time stealing both opportunity and means to declare his own love, lends itself in performance to broad physical humour and slapstick. Lucentio's objection that the music tutor is 'too forward' (l. 1) might be prompted by the sight of physically intimate or sexually suggestive instruction on the part of Hortensio, and at lines 4–15 the argument about the relative priority of music and philosophy might escalate into a literal tug-of-war, the suitors' momentarily all-consuming obsession with each other physicalized with a set of books, a musical instrument, or even Bianca, between them.

16–25   'I'll not be tied to hours'

A new side to Bianca's character emerges, as the modest and obedient daughter of Act II, scene i suddenly shows herself to be forceful,
articulate and able to command. This seeming transformation might
feasibly be explained by the sorts of ideological inconsistencies that
could occur in early modern England when competing hierarchies of
degree and gender made it difficult, even impossible, to determine
the relative status between, for instance, a noble woman and male
tutor. Bianca's domineering manner might likewise be attributed to
the influence of medieval courtly love poetry in which the chaste
mistress was conventionally portrayed as cruel, aloof and unattain-
able, without pity for her suitor, typically figured as her 'servant'.
Nevertheless, her assertion that she will 'not be tied to . . . 'pointed
times' but will rather 'please [her]self' (ll. 19–20) seems less in keeping
with '[m]aid's mild behaviour and sobriety' (I.i.71), than with the
headstrong wilfulness of her sister, Katherina. This is the first indica-
tion that, at least in some circumstances, Bianca, like her elder sister,
is prepared to insist on getting her own way, foreshadowing her
eventual disobedience both to her father and to her husband.

26–53   'Construe them'

The way Lucentio and Bianca alternate between English and Latin
suggests that Hortensio moves in and out of earshot, since the effort
of perpetuating the pretence of oral translation would be otherwise
unnecessary. The precise blocking of the lesson, however, will depend
on details such as the shape of the stage, the production's choice of
instrument (Katherina breaks a lute over his head, but the instrument
taught in this scene could be as large as a double-bass, small as a flute,
or ludicrous as a kazoo), and how suspicious of Lucentio the actors
want the character of Hortensio to seem. Hortensio might remain in
one place always potentially able to hear them, the other two either
elevating their normal speaking voices to read out the Latin, or dropping their voices to a whisper to deliver their clandestine 'translations',
or he might move around the stage while tuning his instrument,
perhaps occasionally trying to sneak up on them. As with asides,
where the convention is that they go unheard by onstage characters
simply if actors take no notice of them, spectators understand

through the actor's facial expressions and body language which lines the character of Hortensio manages to overhear.

This episode provides another perspective on the unruly woman. At the end of the previous scene, Baptista concluded a marriage for his youngest daughter, promising her to his neighbour, Gremio, if Tranio-as-Lucentio is unable within two weeks to make good his assurance. In the very next scene, spectators see Lucentio, in disguise as a Latin tutor, attempt to steal that daughter from her father, not just figuratively, in terms of her heart, but also literally in the sense that she is Baptista's property. Bianca, far from rejecting his advances, tells him to 'despair not' (l. 43), evidently assuming that her future husband, like her hours of schooling, 'resteth in [her] choice' (l. 17). A woman's potential to assert control over her own sexuality – her ability to disobey her father and marry for love – posed an ever-present threat to an early modern socio-economic network founded on careful alliances and prudent marriages. To put this a different way, Katherina may be the most voluble, but she is certainly not the only socially disruptive, female character in *The Taming of the Shrew*.

54–79   'the gamut of Hortensio'

Bawdy sexual puns on the 'instrument' which either/both Hortensio and Bianca will be 'fingering' (l. 63) provide opportunity throughout the music lesson for farcical humour. A strict literary reading of the lesson would suggest that the instrument remains unsounded since Bianca is explicitly cued in the dialogue *not* to pick it up (ll. 62–8). Past productions, however, have taken occasion for Hortensio to accompany Bianca's reading with music, or else for Bianca to sing, rather than read, the gamut, accompanied either by herself or Hortensio. It would be difficult, assuming Bianca reads the letter aloud, and nearly impossible if she sings it, for Lucentio 'really' not to overhear Hortensio's gamut. As with the Latin lesson, however, the third character only hears what the actor feigns to hear – leaving a production to decide how much, or little, of the music lesson a jealous Lucentio will mark.

80–90   'thy wandering eyes'

Hortensio's sententious and judgemental comment on Bianca's 'wandering', 'ranging' behaviour depends on the early modern cultural assumption, elevated here to a form of moral precept, that people should only seek to marry within their own social rank. Richard Jones, writing in his *Heptameron of Civil Discourses* (published in 1582, about ten years before Shakespeare wrote the *Taming of the Shrew*), notes that the problem with trying to combine 'over lofty and too base love' in marriage is that 'spaniels and curs hardly [i.e., with difficulty] live together without snarling'. The problem is not just that Bianca is disloyal to Hortensio's love, or even that she is potentially willing to deceive her father (the success of his own counterfeit disguise, after all, depends on that very possibility), but that she might demean herself by casting her affections on a servant, thus proving, to his mind, the true hollowness of her worth. Once again, and perhaps unexpectedly to modern audiences more attuned to the play's controversial treatment of gender relations, the thematic emphasis falls on a recurrent preoccupation with the transgression of hierarchies of degree.

Act III, scene ii

0   *'Enter . . . Lucentio as Cambio'*

There is no entry cue for Lucentio as Cambio marked in the Folio, but since he speaks with Tranio at line 137, editors often bring him on with the others at the beginning of the scene. If he is onstage from the outset, a production might draw attention to the substitution ploy by staging an unguarded moment when both Tranio and Lucentio answer Baptista in the opening line. Hortensio is not cued in the Folio to enter until the second mass entrance at line 182 (although a production that sets out to create the effect of a grand wedding might decide that his attendance is desirable from the start). The really important choice for performance is whether Hortensio should appear as himself, or in disguise as the music tutor, Licio.

Silent onstage characters can have a major impact on an audience's interpretation of the action. In this scene, for instance, what seems to be Lucentio's response to Tranio's roleplay – is he pleased about, indifferent to, or jealous of his servant's evidently close relationship to Bianca's father? Bianca is probably also present throughout, and even though she already knows about the substitution, she, like the others, has to maintain the pretence that Tranio is really Lucentio and her future husband. If she stands near Tranio, talks privately to him, or otherwise shows him particular favour (as happened in Greg Doran's 2003 Royal Shakespeare Company production), a silent inset love triangle involving master, servant and mistress could be played throughout the scene of Katherina's wedding day that culminates in Baptista telling Bianca and Tranio to fill in at the banquet for the absent bride and groom (ll. 248–9).

1–20   'Lo, there is mad Petruchio's wife'

The laws governing marriage in early modern England were muddy and frequently subject to variable interpretation and abuse. Written documentation of a spousal was not required, and marriage licences were not yet in existence; it was not even absolutely necessary within the state religion of Protestantism for a minister to conduct the ceremony (although it was much preferred). All that was required of a legally binding marriage was an exchange of vows between the couple. It was advisable, however, in case questions should arise later, for others to witness the vows in order to prove that they indeed took place, and many couples would in addition seek the church's blessing and throw a party to celebrate the day.

However, betrothals (also, confusingly, called spousals) could be nearly as binding as actual marriage. If the promise between two people remained conditional on the fulfilment of some stipulation – Tranio-as-Lucentio, for instance, has to get Lucentio's father, or his substitute, to assure his inheritance – then it could be broken off with ease. Otherwise, if it were an unconditional promise sworn with an oath, then, without mutual consent on both sides to annul the contract, each party was legally compelled to marry the other.

Katherina and Petruchio enter into this kind of binding agreement when their hands are joined at II.i.295–313. Katherina never verbally commits herself to do anything other than see him 'hanged on Sunday first' (l. 292), but Petruchio says that when he was alone with her she 'protest[ed] oath on oath' (l. 302). Crucially, this is a claim Bianca's suitors, describing themselves as 'witnesses' to the match (l. 313), are prepared to believe and swear to, thus rendering Petruchio's version of their encounter, if not the factual, then at least the legal, truth. Katherina's wedding day, then, is to some large extent a formality, an opportunity for Baptista's family to show off their wealth and status with rich clothes, a large banquet and many guests.

The unexpected development that Petruchio might never return to claim his betrothed wife is a disaster, not only because it is humiliating for the family, but because Katherina, one half of a legally binding and witnessed contract, cannot with ease enter into a contract of marriage with anyone else. Katherina is cued in the Folio to enter with 'Baptista, Gremio, Tranio . . . Bianca, and others, attendants'. Baptista, his eldest daughter and Tranio are the only ones needed at the beginning of the scene, but a performance choice to gather on stage as many actors as are available to play wedding guests will emphasize the public nature of the family's embarrassment.

21–5   'I know him passing wise'

Tranio has consolidated his place within Baptista's family since agreeing a provisional betrothal to Bianca, and his advice on family affairs is not only sought (l. 7), but given (ll. 21–5). This latter speech might be evidence of clumsy revision since it is impossible for Tranio, a new acquaintance of Petruchio, to 'know him passing wise'. Alternatively, it might more readily be explained as a demonstration of Tranio's inclusion within the family through the sort of 'double time' technique more skilfully evidenced in *Othello* (i.e., an audience accepts that the two men have formed an intimate friendship, even though on closer examination the opportunity for that to have happened does not exist). Another option, and one employed by Monette, is to transfer Tranio's lines to Hortensio, who attends the wedding as himself, and not as the music tutor (see Chapter 4).

In the Induction, the lord anticipated that merely the sight of his men 'do[ing] homage to [a] simple peasant' would be the source of great amusement (Induction 1, l. 133). Precisely that scenario and opportunity for humour is replicated here within the play within the play, Baptista discussing matters seriously with a servant and referring to him as 'Signor Lucentio'. Tranio, however, unlike Sly, seems fully to occupy his new social role and to offer little occasion for laughter in his performance of a nobleman. Whereas the action of the two Inductions reinforces through the spectacle of role-play the social and ideological barriers separating commoners and nobles, that gap between them is blurred, even erased, by Tranio's confident impersonation of Lucentio.

A production that kept Sly and the others onstage to watch the whole of the players' show might seek ways to draw attention at key moments to the contrasting effect of disguise in the separate stories: Tranio and Sly, for instance, might make pointed eye contact; the lord could shuffle nervously on the sidelines, laugh uproariously, or even exit in disapproval; Sly might get up to walk across the stage and examine curiously Tranio's costume, and then his own.

26–9   'Exit weeping'

After Katherina's line at 26, the Folio direction is '*Exit weeping*'. Some editors modify this to '*Exit weeping, followed by Bianca and the other women*'. This cue extends the conflict between bride and groom to the rest of the wedding party, and creates an imagined performance that takes its meaning in part from a perceived gender differentiation: the female characters are visually aligned with Katherina, while the male characters wait around for Petruchio. Allowing Katherina to exit alone, as cued in the Folio, would reinforce a sense of her isolation from the community. Performance, however, might instead choose to interpret Katherina's 'exit' as a cue for her simply to step aside from, or turn her back on, the main action (on the authority of Folio directions, see Chapter 1, pp. 10–11). The bride then could overhear Biondello's report, and witness both Petruchio's entrance and the men's reaction to his costume, either exiting silently at a later point or perhaps rejoining the main group at l. 120.

30–70   'Master, master news!'

This extended description of Petruchio's wedding outfit, his horse's tack and his servant's livery is similar in effect to Hortensio's relation in Act II, scene i of Katherina breaking the lute over his head, in that it builds in advance of an important entry a sense of comic expectation. The humour of Biondello's report, however, unlike the music tutor's account of the failed lesson, relies heavily on an extensive familiarity with the terminology of early modern costume, equine disease and harness. Whereas curious readers may pause to look up the definition of difficult words (and so learn that nobody has been able to recover at lines 66–7 the meaning of 'the humour of forty fancies pricked in't for a feather'), this is not an option available to performance.

A production therefore faces the challenge of how to make these lines meaningful to modern audiences. The actor might try to 'sign' the terminology, indicating as far as possible through physical gesture the visual effect the words describe; the lines might be cut altogether as overly obscure; or the substance of the description might be translated into contemporary cultural references, the actor playing Biondello substituting, for instance, an account of a ramshackle old car for a ramshackle old horse, and patched bell-bottoms for 'a pair of old breeches thrice turned' (l. 44). With this latter option, especially, the goal would be to reproduce in perfor-mance for a modern audience not Shakespeare's words but the effect of those words on his earliest audiences.

Crucially, though, meaning often depends less on what is said than on how it is said. The actor's voice, facial expression and body posture can allow a theatre audience to enjoy the comic energy of the monologue, even if most of the terminology remains unfathomable to twenty-first-century spectators. Especially if Biondello's onstage spectators (Baptista, Tranio, perhaps even Sly and his lady) respond with shock or laughter, the theatre audience will easily grasp the general gist, if not the details, of the passage.

71–83 'Why, sir, he comes not'

The broad comedy of Biondello's lines here and at lines 30–41 depends on a Grumio-like verbal precision that provokes not clarity, but greater confusion, of language (compare I.ii.5–43). The joke at lines 71–83 relies on the misdirections generated by Biondello's insis-tence that it is not Petruchio, but Petruchio and his horse, who comes. His last five lines, whether printed as prose (as in the Folio) or verse, have a lilting, nursery-rhyme quality which reinforces the sense that Biondello and Baptista are working at linguistic cross-purposes.

84–126 'To me she's married, not unto my clothes'

Biondello's advance warning of Petruchio's imminent arrival makes an audience predisposed to find the groom's entrance comic, or at least remarkable, but a major design challenge for those responsible for properties and costume is to decide what exactly Petruchio and Grumio will look like on the wedding day. Their outfits might seem to resemble as closely as possible Biondello's description or, especially if it is a modern-dress production, the designers might instead draw on their imaginations simply to create costumes that seem bizarre and inappropriate for a wedding. Marowitz's Petruchio wore a wedding dress, while in Taylor's production, Petruchio arrived with a boot fitted on his head like a hat (see Chapter 4, p. 124). Biondello also focuses heavily on Petruchio's horse (ll. 48–61) and its accoutrements; it seems unlikely, albeit not impossible, that a live animal would appear on stage either in Shakespeare's time or our own. Past productions have seen Petruchio enter carrying a saddle and harness, or even driving a Vespa dressed up to look like a cartoon horse.

Some editors add 'not' to Petruchio's question at line 90, assuming it has been accidentally omitted during the process of preparing the play for print publication. However, if one infers that Petruchio points to Grumio – or perhaps even to one of the well-dressed guests – at 'thus', the question as printed in the Folio could make good sense in performance. The crucial point is that, whatever he looks like, Petruchio is the outlandish spectacle that draws to him all eyes – he says at lines 93–5 that the guests stare at him as though he were one of the freaks of nature, a 'comet' or 'prodigy', that so fascinated the readers of pamphlets and ballads in the sixteenth and early seventeenth centuries.

Whereas it was previously Katherina who would provide passers-by 'good pastime' (and before her, Sly), now it is Petruchio who is set at the centre of attention, attracting to himself both wonder and disapproval. The Folio only marks exits for Petruchio and Baptista, but an effect of spectacle could be reinforced in performance if their exits were followed by a rowdy exodus of attendants and guests who head off as though to see, not a wedding ceremony, but a circus show or street brawl.

127–47 'But, sir, to love'

The function of this short exchange between Tranio and Lucentio is pragmatic and structural, simply allowing for a space of time sufficient to suggest that the wedding could have been conducted offstage, and thus marking the transition from an anticipation of Petruchio's outrageous wedding gear to the narration of his extraordinary behaviour during the ceremony. Its construction is weak: Tranio implies that he will follow Petruchio (ll. 123–4), but never does, and seems to pick up in the middle of a conversation with Lucentio (l. 127). This may just be an awkwardly written bridge linking the scene's high points, or may be the consequence of a major excision between 126 and 127. Miller solves the problem with a camera cut that suggests a time lapse or scene break (see Chapter 4, p. 134).

148–81 'A grumbling groom'

Gremio's account of the 'grumbling groom' replays an earlier conversation between two of Bianca's suitors (himself and Hortensio), in which Katherina was described as a 'devil', a 'fiend of hell', and told to 'go to the devil's dam' (I.i.66, 88, 105). As the stylized repetition and parallel phrasing at lines 154–5 imply, the infernal qualities attributed previously to Katherina are transferred to Petruchio, confirming Gremio's earlier prediction that only a 'devil' would be fool enough to marry a shrew (I.i.120–2). Although Petruchio clearly has the potential for physical violence – he threatens at II.i.218 to 'cuff' Katherina if she strikes him again – this potential is not realized, insofar as one can tell from the dialogue, against his bride (a production, however, might choose to find occasion for such business). His blows instead seem directed against those around them, such as the priest, and later his own servants. This is a major departure from the shrew-taming literature where plays such as *Tom Tyler and His Wife* (c. 1560), and ballads such as 'A Merry Jest of a Shrewd and Curst Wife' (c. 1550) portray a wife beaten into submission by her husband or his substitute (see Chapter 3, pp. 100–6).

A commonplace device, particularly in film where it is possible to cut quickly from one location to another, is to dramatize reported offstage events such as Gremio's account of the wedding – Taylor stages the wedding (see Chapter 4, p. 124), while Zeffirelli stages both the wedding and Katherina's music lesson. There is no textual authority for these dramatizations, and the dialogue, if there is any, is usually cobbled together from the characters' second-hand reports. The popularity of this performance choice results from the inherent theatricality of the reported action; the language is so vivid, and paints in our minds such a clear picture of what happened, that it becomes almost irresistible to stage the moment, as it were, 'live'.

The downside to such treatments is that they slow the pace of the drama, force spectators to shift among a greater number of more fragmented scenes, and sacrifice the commentary on the action provided by the reporter. Gremio, for instance, corrects Tranio's opinion of the bride – perhaps an opinion shared by the theatre audience – by announcing after the wedding that Petruchio, not Katherina, is 'a devil', and that she is 'a lamb, a dove, a fool to him' (ll. 154–6). If the report is staged rather than told, an audience in effect assumes the position of Gremio, deciding for themselves who is the devil, and who the lamb. The playwright loses the opportunity for external commentary on the action, and control of an audience's evolving perception of character and situation shifts more firmly from the author to the director.

182   'Music plays'

A decision for modern productions, assuming one chooses to follow this cue, is which choice of music might best suit the comedy of the scene, and how it might be performed. The musicians might walk on at the head of the procession playing something traditional, a well-known contemporary love song might be played over the theatre's sound system, or the 'music' might instead consist of a flurry of ill-matched notes sounded by flustered musicians as they are beaten on stage by Petruchio (see Chapter 1, p. 7).

183–205   'I must away'

Petruchio's refusal to stay for the wedding banquet completes his utter disruption of the traditional wedding festivities: he arrived late, dressed inappropriately, beat up the priest and swore at him, drank off the wine and threw the sops in the sexton's face (rather than sharing it among the wedding party, as was the conventional practice), and kissed his bride in an indecorous manner. The strangeness of his decision to leave immediately after the ceremony is highlighted by having three of the most respected male characters (Baptista, Tranio and Gremio), try to convince him to stay. Gremio's near verbal repetition of Tranio's entreaty prepares for Katherina's exact verbal repetition at line 199 of Gremio's line.

A sense of the significance of her intervention, and of her sudden vulnerability – as a woman stepping into conversation among men, as a woman attempting for the first time her influence as a wife, and as a short-tempered fury who never courteously 'entreat[ed]' anything of anyone before – could be drawn out in performance through a short pause before Katherina speaks or a sudden shift in focus caused by her moving from a seated to standing position. Petruchio's Grumio-like quibble, that he is content for her to entreat but not content to stay, is an overt display of his power and authority by seeming at first to concede to her appeal, only to make her the butt of a joke.

206–51 'My horse, my ox, my ass, my anything'

As at Act II, scene i, Katherina at first protests loudly, only to fall suddenly silent. These silences, inexplicable on the page, will inevitably be filled in performance. She may not speak because she is somehow physically silenced by Petruchio or the others, or she may seem either reluctantly or secretly to accept – perhaps even to welcome – Petruchio's authoritative control. There is no direction in the Folio to explain when, how or even if Petruchio grabs his wife to make off with her, and so line 227 ('look not big, nor stamp, nor stare, nor fret') could be read as an intradialogic direction either to Katherina or to the startled wedding party. In the case that nobody 'stamp[s]' and 'stare[s]', it might even be understood as part of Petruchio's histrionic flight of fancy in which he supposes himself 'beset with thieves' (l. 235). A sense of violence and danger could be generated if Petruchio and Grumio draw swords or guns on the guests, or else their get-away could seem farcical if their 'weapons' turn out, for instance, to be plastic toys, or bottles of alcohol. This scene often marks, in modern performance, the end of the first half, and a production that wished to emphasize the onstage confusion as spectators go into intermission might cut lines 239–51, ending the scene with the abrupt departure of the bride and groom.

   Petruchio's claim that he 'will be master of what is [his] own' (l. 228), describing Katherina as his goods and chattels, and likening her to 'My horse, my ox, my ass, my any thing' (l. 231), crudely marks women's precarious legal status as wives in early modern England. After marriage, anything a woman brought to the union became by law the property of her husband. She could retain nothing of her own, and had no legal identity apart from that of her husband except in the case of serious felony (i.e., she could not sue or be sued except in her husband's name, but she remained personally accountable for a crime such as murder). *The Law's Resolution of Women's Rights*, written by 'T.E.' and published in 1632, about forty years after the earliest performances of *The Taming of the Shrew*, explains the powerlessness in law of a married woman (see Chapter 3, pp. 112–13).

ACT IV

Act IV, scene i

1–46   'I am sent before'

If a character enters shivering and calling for a fire, spectators, even at an open-air theatre on a warm summer's afternoon, will gather that within the fiction of the play the temperature is cold. Grumio's account of the journey from Padua tells us that the weather was inhospitable, but it remains uncertain if Petruchio's house is likewise cold and unwelcoming, or if Grumio just says it is. Curtis might eventually kindle a fire on Grumio's repeated command (or, depending on the production's period setting, bring on a brazier of coals, plug in the radiator, or turn up the thermostat), or he might instead point to a fire already burning in a corner of the stage, silently contradicting the need for further heat.

   This is a key scene in modern productions, which are able to take advantage of full set changes and lighting design, as choices have to be made about the appearance of Petruchio's home: it might be tidy or messy, well-managed or neglected, in the style of an elegant estate, wealthy cattle ranch, or derelict shack. This introduction to the home into which Katherina has married can make a strong impact on an audience's perception of character and situation, either confirming or contradicting Petruchio's claim to have 'bettered' the inheritance left to him by his father (II.i.118; see also Chapter 4, p. 135).

46–76 'Tell thou the tale'

Yet again a key entrance – here of Petruchio and Katherina – is anticipated by a long narrative description of offstage action (compare II.i.142–59, III.ii.43–68 and III.ii.156–80). This insistence on the techniques of story-telling is a metatheatrical device that serves to foreground both the way the action unfolds, and different characters' perspective on it, implicitly asking spectators to measure what they are about to see against what they have been told. In keeping with his characteristically farcical engagement with language, Grumio tells his tale by refusing to tell it, paradoxically consigning it to 'oblivion' (l. 74) at the moment of relating it.

77–124 'Are they all ready?'

The precise number of Petruchio's servants is hard to discern from the printed text. In addition to Curtis and Grumio, four servingmen are cued to speak with individual speech prefixes (ll. 95–8), but the Folio imprecisely cues 'four or five Servingmen' to enter (l. 94). This suggests there might be at least one silent onstage presence. 'Peter' eventually gets to speak at l. 166, and between them, Petruchio and Grumio mention the names of six other servants who have no speaking parts (apart from perhaps a collective 'Here sir' at line 109).

Therefore there might be as many as thirteen named servingmen on stage (plus those not explicitly mentioned), or as few as six (or even fewer, if some of the greetings at ll. 95–8 are cut, and Peter's line given to another character). The final number of servants encountered in this scene will vary extensively from one production to another, influenced by the interpretative effect a company hopes to achieve and by pragmatic matters of production resources and decisions about doubling. An important additional consideration for modern performance is whether all of these servants will be played by male actors: Katherina's entrance into an entirely male space, isolated from her family, will suggest different perceptions of potential personal danger than a household comprising men and women.

An opinion about Petruchio's substance and the wealth of his household will inevitably be shaped not only by whether he has many or few serving staff, but by how they look and behave. This last point poses yet another textually indeterminate problem, since conflicting evidence is offered about the servants' readiness. Curtis and Nathaniel confirm that 'All things is ready' (l. 103, see also l. 85), but Petruchio declares on entering that everything is at sixes and sevens, a claim Grumio seems readily to confirm. Are Petruchio's house and servants in order, or not? Does Katherina enter a slovenly, ill-cared-for bachelor flat, or is it a well-appointed and immaculate residence?

Either the servants are telling the truth or Petruchio is, which implies that one could interpret the scene either way – crucially, however, whereas a reader may weigh both options simultaneously, a production has to choose one or the other. If the house seems a mess or the servants incompetent, an audience might be led to assume that Petruchio is a poor domestic manager, or that he deceived Baptista about his wealth, either of which options might seem variously horrifying and/or comic to an audience who considers the situation from Katherina's perspective. On the other hand, if the house seems beautifully kept, then Petruchio would seem wilfully perverse, an option which would be in keeping with his behaviour in the previous scene, but perhaps no more encouraging for Katherina.

125–35   'Sit down, Kate, and welcome.'

Although cued to enter with Petruchio at line 105, Katherina does not speak for nearly forty lines; indeed, she is not even addressed for twenty lines. This raises the possibility that they might not enter together. In Greg Doran's 2003 Royal Shakespeare Company production, Petruchio suddenly seemed to remember that he has a wife and went to fetch her from offstage as late as line 128. If she enters with her husband, the actor playing the part will have to decide what to do while he shouts at his servants.

Katherina's relative silence throughout this scene – she speaks only twice, for a total of three lines – means not that she will be an insignificant stage presence, but that spectators curious to mark her earliest response to the 'taming school' have to infer that reaction from the actor's bearing and facial expressions, the state of her costume, and what she does throughout Petruchio's interactions with his servants. She might stand stunned at the back of the stage until invited by Petruchio to '[s]it down' at line 128 (or continue to stand at a distance from the main action); she might enter to collapse in exhaustion at a table; or she might begin to tidy the room, unpacking some things she brought from Padua. Introducing business with a whip would make Petruchio's presence in this scene seem even louder, and more violent and intimidating (see Chapter 4, p. 121).

136–8   'Where's my spaniel Troilus?'

Animal imagery runs throughout this play with dogs, horses, wasps, crabs, falcons, and the behaviours or activities associated with these creatures, threaded through much of the characters' language. Petruchio promises to 'tame' Katherina, evidently as he would domesticate any other animal, bringing her 'from a wild Kate to a Kate / Conformable as other household Kates' (II.i.269–71). The introduction of Troilus in terms of a question about his absence means that a dog need never appear on stage. However, it seems a possibility, especially since we know Shakespeare's company occasionally brought dogs on stage: *The Two Gentlemen of Verona*, for example, another early comedy which scholars date just prior to *The Taming of the Shrew*, includes scenes for a servant, Lance, and his 'cruel-hearted cur', Crab.

Animals in performance can be scene-stealers, and careful thought would have to go into what kind of dog Petruchio might own. A spaniel is a fairly neutral indoor breed, but a hound, for example, might suggest the hunt and so emphasize Petruchio's masculinity, a pitbull terrier or doberman might imply brutality, while a tiny chihuahua with a red bow (especially one called 'Troilus') might seem comically incongruous. Grumio carried in a King Charles spaniel in Miller's production; Taylor, by contrast, had Petruchio deliver his soliloquy at the end of the scene to a Great Dane. Both of these, significantly, are filmed productions. On a purely pragmatic level, a live production that brings a dog on stage increases the chance of unexpected, even unwelcome, incidents. This, however, might be considered an acceptable risk, as shared knowledge of that very possibility adds to the farce, generating a certain metatheatrical energy between stage and audience.

Another potential silent presence in this scene is that of Petruchio's 'cousin Ferdinand' whom Katherina 'must kiss and be acquainted with' (l. 138). The line could easily be overlooked in a busy scene (or cut), but staged performance often creates striking effects and startling new insights into character and situation by picking up on precisely this kind of loose end. Who is cousin Ferdinand, will he have a theatrical existence beyond this one line, and if so, why does he not speak? Gesture, costume and stage business could all build without words various identities for this character, such as Petruchio's hostile gay lover or a disabled relative for whom Petruchio cares and provides shelter (see Chapter 4, p. 140).

139–64   'He strikes the Servant'

The Folio includes directions for servants to enter 'with supper' and 'with water' (ll. 128, 135), but no cues for Petruchio to strike his servants (ll. 133, 141), to 'knock the basin out of the Servant's hands' (l. 140), or to 'throw the food and dishes at them' (l. 151). As with the whip, stage tradition has made this sort of business commonplace, and so modern editors often introduce it into the printed text as the obvious, even necessary, physical accompaniment to the aggression of Petruchio's words. However, in the same manner one might question how the sight of Sly drinking a lot or a little in the second induction modifies one's view both of Sly and of the lord who dismisses him as a 'drunkard', one might probe here the interpretative function of either less, or more, violence.

The key question is how a production presents this scene fitting into the larger context of the taming process. Violence could be used to reinforce a production's slapstick humour, with dishes, tables and pans flying all over the stage; it could serve as a reminder of the lessons of the shrew-taming tracts, that headstrong women are 'cured' of their behaviour through beatings; or the details of Petruchio's actions could be made to coincide as closely as possible with Katherina's behaviour in one of her earlier scenes, shaming her, as it were, with the mirror of her own short-tempered anger (for more on this so-called 'therapy' technique, see Chapter 4, pp. 134–6). This last option, in particular, implies that Petruchio lashes out at his servants as part of a deliberate and controlled performance designed to tame Katherina, a feigned show that may have started as early as the wedding scene in Padua.

A production might instead trouble an interpretation of Petruchio as the overbearing master by having him, for instance, yell constantly but ineffectually at his overbearing servants, or by showing him unable, or unwilling, to keep up the façade of an irascible domestic tyrant by establishing a contrast between Petruchio's abusive words and kind actions (for instance, behind Katherina's back he might pick up and return to the servant the basin he has accidentally let fall). David Garrick gave an extra line to one of the servants to make it explicit that this extreme behaviour is uncharacteristic of Petruchio (see Chapter 4, p. 122). These alternative stagings to the imagined editorial performance, while by no means necessary, might offer a more complex reading of character, and present as far less certain the eventual outcome of the contest between Katherina and Petruchio.

165–73   'Peter, didst ever see the like?'

The 'Exeunt' and 'Enter Servants severally' at line 164, both of which stage directions are printed in the Folio, suggest the unusual situation where the stage is empty of characters for a moment in the middle of a scene. The effect of the servants entering 'severally' (separately, from different directions) might be of characters coming out from under cover, and it seems feasible that instead of making an entrance from offstage, they might reappear from behind doors, under tables, or from other hiding spaces onstage. Their short exchange serves two purposes. First, the servants act as a sort of fearful chorus to the action that has passed, prompting spectators to share with them a view of Petruchio's behaviour as unusual and strange. Secondly, Curtis's report provides further, more concise evidence of his master's 'mad-brain' conduct (III.ii.10), by telling us about his 'sermon of continency' (l. 169), without, however, actually requiring the actors to stage it.

174–95   'This is a way to kill a wife with kindness'

This is the second time the possibility of Katherina's death arises (compare l. 166), and one of the moments when the spectre of tragedy intrudes itself on the action's humour. Wives thought to be disobedient or unruly were frequently killed by their husbands on the early modern stage: one thinks here of *Othello*, or even, especially through its parallel use of the proverbial expression 'to kill a wife with kindness' (l. 194), Thomas Heywood's *A Woman Killed with Kindness*, a play about an adulterous wife who starves herself to death after her 'kind' husband learns of her illicit affair, and banishes her from their family and household. Critics disturbed by the sexual politics of *The Taming of the Shrew* have long been tempted to categorize it not as a farce or romantic comedy, but as a 'troubling comedy' or 'light tragedy' (see Chapter 6, pp. 152–6).

This soliloquy, in which Petruchio bluntly articulates the strategy by which he plans to compel obedience from his wife – to deny her food and sleep, as he would an untrained falcon, until she conforms to his will – lies at the heart of the critical debate surrounding the play. In effect Petruchio determines to win a power struggle between husband and wife through what we would now consider a form of psychological torture, always presenting his attentions, in a manner not dissimilar to his overt manipulation of language in Act II, scene i, as 'reverend care of her' (l. 190). Some critics argue that Petruchio is doing Katherina a favour, releasing her from the social isolation caused by her ill-tempered behaviour; others interpret the drama as a farce in which, by definition, characters are incapable of emotional or physical harm. Nonetheless, a persistent uneasiness about an evident readiness on the early modern stage to kill wives physically or spiritually, whether through kindness or other available means, has made this play one of Shakespeare's more politically volatile dramas (see especially the discussion of Charles Marowitz's staging in Chapter 4, pp. 127–31).

196–7   'Now let him speak'

These last two lines offer the actor a choice of performance styles. Soliloquies are often played nowadays as opportunities to develop an effect of interiority, the sense that theatre audiences have privileged access to the inner workings of a character's intentions and inner thinking. However, actors on Shakespeare's earliest open-air stages probably shifted fluidly between a presentational and representational mode of delivery, sometimes remaining within the fictional space, but at other times overtly acknowledging the presence of spectators (see Chapter 1, p. 8). The question, then, for modern performance is whether Petruchio will bridge the divide that separates stage and auditorium by directly addressing the theatre audience, and even seeming to wait for an answer to his demand. The tactic of appealing to the audience's experience and seeking its advice momentarily breaks the fiction, but it carries the potential to make even disapproving spectators feel suddenly complicit with Petruchio and his taming strategies.

Act IV, scene ii

1–5   'Is't possible, friend Licio?'

Act IV is characterized by scenic disjunction, as Shakespeare keeps two, now very separate, plots simultaneously in motion. The act is structured as a series of five scenes, and the audience's attention shifts in turn from Katherina's taming at Petruchio's home in Verona to the courtship of Bianca in Padua. The beauty of this framework is that the romantic fortunes of the two sisters are divided, both in terms of geography and dramatic action, after the wedding scene at the end of Act III, only to dovetail again at the top of Act V, when Petruchio and Katherina deliver Vincentio, the real father, to Lucentio's door. The bibliographical irony that attends this perceived structural and interpretative order is that it depends on editorial emendation to tame the unruly Folio. An otherwise very lightly divided Folio text marks 'Actus Quartus. Scena Prima' (i.e., Act IV, scene i), contrarily placing it at the head of what we now, conventionally, identify as Act IV, scene iii (the tailor's scene).

6–10   'Stand by and mark'

This scene offers yet another example of a play within a play within a play, with Lucentio and Bianca unwittingly providing a show of love for their unseen spectators, Hortensio and Tranio (compare

I.i.46–54 and I.ii.138–60). While they are watched, the two lovers engage in gentle stichomythic wordplay that turns on the opposition of 'master' (the man in power, a tutor, and a holder of an advanced university degree) and 'mistress' (the woman in power, and female object of Lucentio's affections). These may be the first words the actors playing Lucentio and Bianca address to each other upon entering the stage, or, especially if the two groups of characters walk on stage at the same time from separate entrances, we may instead, with Hortensio and Tranio, seem secretly to pick up on their conversation in mid-flow. The words of the scorned suitors at lines 27 and 34 imply that the spectacle of Bianca and her lover continues in silence, their illustrative example and the others' commentary on it framing the emblem of 'unconstant womankind' (l. 14).

A question for performance is to decide what Bianca and Lucentio do in silence until Hortensio exits at line 43. The lovers may talk privately, kiss and cuddle, have sex – or they may even just read their books, thus distancing Bianca from her onstage audience's estimation of her as a whore by comically demonstrating how Hortensio and Tranio interpret her behaviour as suits their own personal and political agenda. Monette had the lovers step offstage, but still evidently within sight of Tranio and Hortensio; Tranio's and Hortensio's head movements as they seemed to watch Bianca and Lucentio was comically suggestive of contorted sexual positions.

11–35 'I am called Hortensio'

There is no equivalent to the figure of Hortensio in Gascoigne's *Supposes* (see Chapter 3, p. 95). This character is consistently useful to Shakespeare in terms of the way he links the disguise and taming plots. Hortensio interests Petruchio in Katherina and her money, and provides him with means of access to Baptista. Later, as a second master-in-disguise, he serves as the comic butt of both daughters' music lessons, a function less readily filled by Lucentio, the suitor who will eventually win Bianca in marriage (but see Chapter 4 for early stagings in which the characters of Hortensio and Lucentio were conflated). Then in the final scene he and his widow make a third married couple, drawing out the wager and so helping to create as a dramatic effect a sense of shocked wonder at the sight of

Katherina's transformation. Unlike Gremio, who will remain a bachelor spectator to the wager, and who is therefore free to pursue to the
frustrated end his suit to Bianca, Hortensio has to renounce his claim
to the younger daughter and marry the widow, '[e]re three days pass'
(l. 38) – which, from a playwright's consideration of plot structure, is
as much as to say before the impromptu second wedding banquet.

This passage therefore provides occasion for the rejection of
Bianca. Hortensio's objection to her supposed infidelity rests on a
perception of the travesty of degree and societal impropriety implicit
in upstart servants and undiscerning mistresses. Like Hamlet, who
accuses his mother of leaving 'this fair mountain' to 'batten on this
moor' (*Hamlet*, III.iv.65–6), Hortensio attacks Bianca's lack of discre-
tion in 'leav[ing] a gentleman' to make 'a god of such a cullion' (ll.
19–20; cullion was another word for 'testicle', and so came to be used
at this time as a term of insult). The scene of Hortensio's disavowal of
his mistress also partakes of Hamlet's misogyny, since Hortensio and
Tranio, the two disappointed suitors, find in the supposed moral
frailty of one woman a condition universal to womankind.

The joke, of course, is that Hortensio seeks to police boundaries of
degree, signified and enforced in everyday discourse through regula-
tions of costume, within the heightened theatrical context of a lord in
disguise as a servant (Hortensio) telling a servant in disguise as a lord
(Tranio) that his mistress is being wooed by a servant (who is actually
Lucentio, another lord in disguise). In a moment of dramatic irony,
Hortensio wishes on Bianca at line 35 precisely the 'ill' fortune that
Tranio has been trying to facilitate since his arrival in Padua, that all
but his master, Lucentio, would 'quite forsw[ear]' her.

36–43   'a wealthy widow'

This is the first mention of another possible marriage candidate for
Hortensio, and she is identified only by her marital status, never by a
personal name. Her condition as a widow is of immense thematic
importance to a play which is so heavily invested in the intercon-
nectedness of marriage and money. Widows in early modern drama
are typically presented as headstrong and sexually lewd (see l. 50), a
stock characterization that articulates anxieties about the unique
independence of their real-life counterparts in English society. One

of the few ways women could have access to money as their own, and hold property and assets in their own name was through a husband's death. With the death of a husband, a woman would come into what could be a substantial inheritance (the jointure bestowed on her at marriage, plus any additional land and goods bestowed on her in her dead husband's will). On remarriage, this wealth would pass to her second husband unless it was entailed, in which case it would either return to her first husband's family estate or devolve to her children. However, for a period of time – as long, indeed, as she chose to remain unmarried – this woman (who was potentially quite young, if one thinks of the hypothetical scenario of Bianca marrying Gremio) was legally free to manage her own finances and sexuality.

The widow could thus seem, to an early modern patriarchal imagination, the very embodiment of fears about ungoverned womanhood, and the professional (male) playwrights responded to this threat by transforming her on the stage into an unruly figure of fun. The widow in *The Taming of the Shrew* is not only independently wealthy but, evidently having no father or brother to control her will, negotiates a second marriage for herself. The contrast among the three brides is telling and ironic. The widow arranges her own marriage, Bianca elopes with her lover – only Katherina, ostensibly the play's titular 'shrew' and supposed transgressor of patriarchal authority, is passed from father to husband in an orderly way. The introduction of this unnamed bride for Hortensio thus sets the stage for the ultimate exhibition of male priority and female submission wherein the reformed shrew confronts as inappropriate to their sex, the manifest licence (and licentiousness) of the widow and the runaway.

44–71   'Nay, I have ta'en you napping, gentle love'
Tranio remains the dominant figure throughout this scene – he listens to Hortensio's revelation of Bianca's infidelity and swears with him an oath to abandon her, he tells the two lovers they have been caught unawares, and he sets up the Pedant as his supposed father. He increasingly comes to occupy a space and linguistic register less in keeping with a servant than a master. Notably, although Tranio addresses Bianca within courtly conventions as his 'mistress' and

'gentle love', the status differential between himself and Lucentio never arises, and while it remains a choice for performance whether Biondello addresses Lucentio or Tranio as 'master' at line 59 and again at line 63, it is Tranio who answers to the title.

There arises the possibility then that not just Baptista and Biondello, but also Bianca, might take the man for the master. There is nothing in the dialogue to suggest that Tranio might admire Bianca, or that Bianca might consider Tranio anything more than Lucentio's helpful servant, yet precisely this interpretation could be conveyed through decisions about physical proximity, whether and how the two of them touch each other, eye contact (or avoidance of eye contact), and tone of voice. Performance, in other words, creates the appearance of relative intimacy or formality through nuanced physical interaction that inevitably exceeds the spoken (or read) word. Hortensio exits this scene believing Bianca is an unfaithful mistress; performance choices subsequent to his departure could seem either to confirm or deny his misgivings.

72–121   'you are like to Sir Vincentio'
This encounter with the character who will substitute for Vincentio, Lucentio's father, and the elaborate fiction by means of which Tranio enlists him to their cause (ll. 81–7) derive from a scene in Gascoigne's *Supposes* (see Chapter 3, pp. 95–100). Shakespeare transformed this long narrative sequence into two separate scenes of enacted spectacle. One falls here in scene ii, and the other, the 'auction' of Bianca that concludes with Tranio's decision to find a 'supposed' father for a 'supposed' son, at the end of Act II, scene i.

Act IV, scene iii
1–14   'did he marry me to famish me?'
The way the playwright alternates scenes in Verona with scenes in Padua generates in both plots a perception of time passing. Spectators returning to Verona after the break provided by the action of Act IV, scene ii assume that Katherina's experiences since her introduction to her new home have been on-going; they merely pick up the thread of the taming narrative at some indeterminate moment – perhaps the

next day, or perhaps the day before Bianca's wedding, nearly a week later. This effect of a marked temporal shift is reinforced by the way the scene opens with Grumio's reply to Katherina's unheard question, their entry *in media res* suggesting a pre-history that is independent of the action spectators witnessed in Act IV, scene i. This dramaturgical manipulation of time implicitly draws attention to the physical appearance of Katherina, and how it might have altered as a consequence of her stay at the 'taming school'.

A production might, for instance, use costuming, voice and gesture to create the sense that Petruchio's home in the country is, for Katherina, more like a prison; a creative team might even decide to introduce make-up effects (a black eye, a raw welt across the arm, a swollen lip) to suggest that Petruchio's taming methods are not exclusive of physical abuse (see Chapter 4, pp. 127–36, for a discussion of Charles Marowitz's and Jonathan Miller's staging of the Verona scenes). Alternatively, and more in keeping with the conventions of farce, there may be little or no evidence of long-term or even short-term damage, with Petruchio's 'kindnesses', and Katherina's anger, remaining entirely the stuff of comedy. Katherina's opening speech, which might be spoken to Grumio, or else played to the audience almost in the manner of a soliloquy, is the counterpoint to Petruchio's soliloquy at the end of scene i, and marks how his promised behaviour has been transformed into her now familiar homelife.

15–51   'I thank you, sir'

This long scene is structured as a series of material goods first offered but then denied to Katherina: food, a cap, a gown, a trip to her father's house. The way Grumio taunts Katherina is crude, and consists simply of summoning up in language a delicious meal, only to reject it on medical grounds as 'too hot' or choleric (humours theory taught that temperament was determined by the particular balance of blood, phlegm, choler and black bile in one's body, and that choler – excessive anger – could be alleviated through diet). Petruchio takes his servant's display of power – the authority to decide for Katherina what is best for her – one step further, by actually bringing on stage in turn the objects of desire.

That this interaction seeks to infantilize Katherina, to make visible her humiliation and subjection, is made explicit at the moment Petruchio demands thanks before allowing his wife to eat the meal he has prepared; the food becomes the tamer's bait as he fabricates a public stand-off that the hungry Katherina has no choice but to back down from. An important interpretative point concerns the manner of her submission, as spectators mark both how long at lines 46–7 the actors extend the silence between husband and wife, and how exactly the actor playing Katherina eventually gives thanks, whether in despair, sarcastically or through gritted teeth. Hortensio's reproof of Petruchio – the bystander stepping in momentarily, and perhaps unexpectedly, to offer support to one he earlier described as 'shrewd and froward' (I.ii.89) – seems on the page to refer to the battle of wills he is being forced to witness, a battle made unequal by Petruchio's exclusive access to the kitchens. In performance, however, his sudden outburst could be prompted by something much more specific, such as Petruchio starting to throw the food away, slapping his wife, or even in his frustration striking Hortensio.

52–9   'What, has thou dined?'

The comedy of this passage in performance is usually that Katherina, finally provided with food and told to 'eat apace' (l. 52), still goes without, Hortensio obeying Petruchio's instruction to '[e]at it up all' (l. 50). The challenge in the theatre is to find sufficient cause for Katherina not to eat at all, or else very little, while Petruchio delivers a long, one-sentence description of the finery in which they will return to Padua. Petruchio might forcibly hold her away from the food, or perhaps she might be distracted from the meal by his ostentatious account of expensive clothing and accessories. However it is staged, this moment shows Katherina, to paraphrase her account of Grumio's verbal tactics, 'f[ed] with the very name of [clothing]' (l. 32). Alternatively, a performance in which Hortensio enabled Katherina to eat something would trouble not just a traditional theatrical interpretation, but also Petruchio's taming methods, and the male bonds of friendship and service that implicitly unite Hortensio, Grumio and Petruchio against Katherina. In this latter imagined staging, the comedy of Petruchio's question, 'What, has thou dined?' would result from his dismay, not hers, about who has consumed the food.

60–85   'Why, thou say'st true'

This argument about the value of the cap is reminiscent of the way Petruchio counters in Act II, scene i Katherina's opposition to their marriage. Language can offer her no recourse from his 'kindness' since in an environment where Petruchio controls the meaning of words, speech is ineffectual. His response at lines 81–3, praising his wife for agreeing with his estimation of the cap, simply ignores the substance of her demand to hold and articulate her own opinions, while at line 86 he seems to mishear 'gown' for 'none', so utterly disempowering her emphatic, rhetorically poised, monosyllabic ultimatum. Significantly, apart from a three-line interjection to confirm that she considers the gown as fashionable as the cap (thus making it clear to Petruchio, and to the audience, that he takes from her something she desires), Katherina falls silent for the rest of her fitting. The actor playing this role will probably remain on the stage, an important visual focus, with her countenance and demeanour conveying any number of a range of emotions (see Chapter 4, p. 140, for the way this scene anticipated in Monette's production the sun–moon scene and the moment of Katherina's submission).

86–100   'she's like to have neither cap nor gown'

Katherina tells us that she has been prevented from eating and sleeping, and troubled with constant brawling (ll. 9–10), but what the audience actually witnesses is Petruchio denying his wife the means to dress fashionably. This extended sequence with the tailor provides the occasion to display Petruchio's techniques of social conditioning without, however, necessarily seeming to transform comedy into something darker and more disturbing. Ladies' tailors were comic figures on the early modern stage, closely related to the figure of the fop or dandy, another character whose masculinity was brought into question through his excessive, and so unmanly, interest in fashionable appearances, conspicuous consumption, and women's bodies. Because they were considered womanish – it proverbially took three (or nine) tailors to make a man – tailors were also seen as prone to debauchery.

A 'tailor scene' therefore had ready-made comic potential in terms of sexual innuendo and the spectacle of failed masculinity. The opportunities for physical comedy are numerous, and performance choices often include Petruchio tearing the gown to shreds or berating a cowering tailor. Whereas the joke on the early modern stage, as Grumio makes clear at lines 153–9, was that the lecherous tailor might have sex with his female customers and so cuckold their husbands, the comedy surrounding the tailor on the modern stage tends to rely on homophobic cultural stereotypes about gay men.

The strategy of gaining control through deprivation may at first seem trivialized by a dramatic method that substitutes the tailor's clothing for Katherina's body as the focus of Petruchio's violent attack. However, by mocking as impractical and ridiculously extravagant the fine clothing Katherina desires, Petruchio sets in place an implicit ideological opposition between (her and the tailor's) luxurious effeminacy and (his) manly restraint. It matters a great deal, in other words, that the husband happens to attack his wife's richly decorated costume, because by this means he not only disciplines her tongue and body (as in the ballads), but displays his own capacity for masculine reason by correcting her evident vulnerability to temptation and excess. The contest for patriarchal control that lies behind their seemingly petty disagreements about fashionable tastes thus marks, at least in part, an assertion of the priority of manhood by locating as the site of misogynist slapstick humour anything – a silk cap, a curiously stitched gown, an effeminate tailor, an unruly wife – that might seem potentially to compromise it.

101–59   'Face not me'
Like Gremio at II.i.293, the tailor briefly becomes Katherina's advocate and Petruchio's opponent in this battle of wills by correcting his paraphrase of her language. Whereas Petruchio's achievement in that earlier scene was to convince the other men to accept, if not necessarily believe, that he and Katherina are saying the same thing, in this scene an abusively worded, but imprecisely motivated, accusation at line 106–13 that the tailor 'liest' (he lies about what?) allows Petruchio to shift the subject of their conflict from his wife's opinion back to the construction of the gown. Katherina and her views on the gown

fall out of the argument altogether, as she silently witnesses with the audience how the tailor's language, both spoken and written, becomes subject to the same sort of misprision, error and bawdy wordplay with which she is forced to live, the complete failure of communication around 'cut' sleeves at lines 139–46 prompting finally the threat of physical violence.

A 'cut' in the context of sixteenth-century fashion refers to a slash that was cut into an outer layer of material so that the fabric underneath, often of a contrasting colour, could show through. These slashes or cuts – particularly popular for the enormous, padded sleeve called a 'trunk sleeve' (l. 137), but also used to decorate doublets, bodices and shoes – could be of varying lengths and were usually arranged in an attractive pattern. The instruction that the 'sleeves [should be] curiously cut' (l. 139) thus details an elaborate and ostentatious style of surface decoration to which Petruchio takes offence. Grumio plays on the less specialized sense of 'cut' to insist that the bill tells the tailor to cut *out* in fabric the shape of the sleeves, before sewing the pieces together to create the finished article.

Not only Grumio's sartorial wordplay, but Petruchio's precise objection to the expensive gown, would be lost on a spectator unaware of 'cutting' as a trendy fashion. This is a real problem for modern performance, and perhaps explains why it is so common now to see Petruchio grab hold of one of the cuts (thus pointing out to an audience the source of his displeasure) and tear the sleeves off the dress, before going on to destroy the rest of the gown. Such stage business may or may not have been incorporated into the earliest performances of the tailor's scene. As with Petruchio's warning that he is prepared to 'cuff' his wife if she strike him again (II.i.218), this interpolated violence implicitly harkens back to the brutality of the more usual shrew-taming methods.

160–4 'I'll pay thee . . . tomorrow'

Asides are printed in Shakespeare's drama only very occasionally, and the Folio marks none in this scene. Editors introduce them where they think, whether for reasons of decorum, situation or consistency of characterization, that it does not make good sense for one or more lines to be heard by every character on stage. In this way, they shape a particular interpretation of the action – an imagined staging – that might not be shared by all readers. Here, editorial asides indicate that Petruchio's disclosure that the tailor will be paid for his gown remains secret to both Hortensio and the tailor, as well as the theatre audience. This staging permits, if only briefly and surreptitiously, the reassertion of a linguistically stable world to which Petruchio conforms. It is kept hidden from Katherina presumably because payment seems – and would seem to Katherina – an implicit acknowledgement that the tailor's interpretation of the bill is correct.

The choice not to deliver these lines as asides might seem to confirm, by contrast, that Petruchio, regardless of whether he is satisfied with the product, honours his financial obligations without, however, conceding to anyone – Hortensio, the tailor, or even the spectators – that his linguistic construction of Katherina's reality is not omnipotent. How powerful is Petruchio? When, if ever, does he step back from a joke taken too far? These are the sorts of interpretative questions that will be answered one way or another – albeit rarely ever in quite the same way twice – in performance.

165–92   'It shall be seven'

This particular disagreement between Katherina and Petruchio marks a new strategic departure in their relationship. Before first meeting his future wife, Petruchio determined to interpret all of her words in a contrary sense (II.i.168–80), a tactic he pursues early in this scene with regard to her opinion about the cap and the gown. However, when he insists that Katherina must concur with his grossly incorrect telling of the time, Petruchio moves beyond the use of language as a means to disempower and disregard her woman's voice, to insist that she will ratify as true any arbitrary relation, no matter how absurd, he seeks to establish between language and the world around them. Language suddenly becomes, not the tool by which Petruchio undercuts his wife's domineering manner, but the acid test through which he tests her continued subjection.

The game has changed, and a quiet life for Katherina now depends on obeying her husband even when she knows he is flatly wrong. Petruchio's assertion of a seemingly contradictory relation between authority, truth and obedience was already familiar to early modern

English subjects. The *Homily against Disobedience and Wilful Rebellion*, delivered periodically throughout the calendar year in local churches, taught that it is a damnable sin for subjects to rise up against even an immoral, unjust or tyrannical ruler, as he or she is God's minister on earth (see Chapter 3, pp. 110–12). In a culture in which analogies between the sovereignty of state and home were commonplace, the inference is obvious: Petruchio, king of his own domestic castle, requires of his wife the same absolute obedience demanded by monarchs of subjects.

Act IV, scene iv

1–17   'Imagine 'twere the right Vincentio'

The casting and costuming of the Pedant are important issues for performance because this character's extremely limited functional role – an imposter who stands in for an absent father – encourages spectators to interpret his place within the action relationally, by measuring him against what he is not. Biondello chose him in Act IV, scene ii out of all the other passers-by in the road, not because of what he *is* (he vaguely speculates he might be a merchant or pedant), but because of what he *seemed*: 'formal in apparel, / In gait and countenance surely like a father' (ll. 63–5).

Therefore, from the moment he walks on stage in IV.ii, spectators examine his costume and bearing to assess Biondello's choice, and to determine if he really is a likely substitute for Vincentio. One's impression of him will be formed in an instant, and will be shaped by any number of theatrical choices including accent, age, hairstyle and/or hat, whether or not he wears a beard and glasses, or walks with a cane, whether he is dressed in a three-piece suit or patched jeans (on the Folio's direction for the Pedant to enter 'booted and bare headed' see Chapter 1, p. 6). The less like a grave 'father' this character appears, the more comic will seem Tranio's task to transform him into the supposed Vincentio.

When the Pedant next appears, here in this scene, his entry 'like Vincentio' begs from spectators a sort of before-and-after comparison as they measure how much he has changed from his first appearance two scenes earlier. Once again, costume and bearing are crucial:

he might look entirely the same, suggesting perhaps that Biondello's choice was apt, or he could be completely (or, more comically, only partly and ineptly) transformed into something better resembling Lucentio's rich father. The moment when the two Vincentios confront each other (V.i.14) finally gives spectators the opportunity to draw direct comparisons between the two men. The similarity or disparity of the actors' bodies, faces and costuming will help to shape a sense of this plot complication as pure farce – if, for instance, the imposter suddenly seems ludicrously unconvincing – or a serious problem of confused identity, and so, especially for Vincentio threatened with prison, something potentially more dangerous.

18–67   'stand good father to me now'

The Pedant's impersonation of Vincentio begins with Baptista's entrance, a moment of dramatic irony and suspense that reprises Tranio's entry as Lucentio in I.ii, with both onstage and theatre audiences curiously waiting to see if his performance will be sufficiently convincing to gull Baptista. His opening address to Baptista is printed in the Folio as one long run-on sentence. Most modern editions adapt this speech by putting 'Soft, son!' on its own line (perhaps thus creating a pause approximately equal in length to four feet of verse, during which time the Pedant turns his attention from his 'son' to Baptista), and breaking the speech into a series of shorter sentences. This treatment of lineation and punctuation, while poetically and grammatically improving the lines, blurs for a reader the potential effect in performance of the Pedant rushing (like a nervous actor?) through a poorly prepared speech.

68   'Enter Peter'

A direction such as this – an entry for a new character who has no speaking lines, and no discernible function – speaks to everything that remains unknown about the textual provenance and earliest performances of The Taming of the Shrew (see Chapter 1, pp. 1–5). Editors tend to describe him in the stage direction as 'a Servingman', implying that he enters to tell Tranio (silently) that a meal awaits him at Lucentio's house, but this is more than we know. Such an invitation is certainly unnecessary from the perspective of plot construction. Other scholars suggest that 'Peter' might be the name of an actor in Shakespeare's company, perhaps the same actor who turns up as a servingman in the Verona scenes (see IV.i.165–6). Alternatively, this stage direction – like the two separate cues to describe the Pedant's appearance earlier in the scene – might point to the sort of glitch sometimes caused by a 'false start' on the author's part, or inept or incompletely executed textual revision.

Uncertainties about the relation of *A Shrew* to *The Shrew*, and speculation that the former might represent some type of corrupt version of the other, tends, paradoxically, to reinforce the view that here something has gone wrong or that something is missing in the 'good' text. This is the same reasoning that, in its extreme version, is used to suggest that the Sly material in *The Shrew* must be incomplete since, in contrast to *A Shrew*, the tinker disappears after I.i (see Chapter 1, pp. 3–4). Over four hundred years on, Peter is the ghostly presence who will not go, or be explained, away. He remains as a silent testament to the instability of early modern printed texts, and the ephemerality of early modern performance.

69–74 *'Exeunt'*

The Folio marks an exit for Biondello at line 67, an entrance for Lucentio and Biondello at line 72, but no exit for Lucentio. Editors tend to infer a missing exit for Lucentio, and introduce it after Baptista's speech (ll. 62–6). The imagined page performance is thus that the two servants (Lucentio and Biondello) are sent on errands by their masters; the stage is cleared of actors; then both servants enter, Biondello catching up with Lucentio to explain Tranio's device. Even though there is a cleared stage, few editions (with the exception of the Oxford *Complete Works*) mark the re-entrance of the servants as a new scene. The source of this oversight, perhaps better described now as editorial convention, dates back to George Steevens who, in 1773, was the first editor to introduce into this play scene breaks.

Perhaps, however, Steevens' reluctance to add a new scene was more cautious than careless, since instead of adding an exit and a scene break, it seems equally feasible that editors might simply remove the exit for Biondello at l. 67, or reinterpret it as a 'stalled' exit, Biondello standing to one side until he is able to have a private word with Lucentio after the others leave. Therefore, in performance this sequence might be interpreted as either a new scene or continuous action, the choice for actors being whether it seems preferable for reasons of pace, characterization or stage space to imply that Biondello and Lucentio shift their location before entering into dialogue (see Chapter 4, p. 139 for Monette's decision to stage their dialogue over the telephone).

75–104 'a wench married in an afternoon'

Elopement, difficult to distinguish in early modern English laws from abduction, was in effect property theft against the woman's father. Baptista is prepared to give his daughter in marriage to the man he thinks is Lucentio, but the legal settlement they are agreeing, signed by the 'deceiving father of a deceitful son' (l. 80) is fraudulent, and so worthless. The only way Lucentio can win Bianca, and so elude the 'hearkening' Gremio (l. 53), is through theft. This illegal but relative straightforward means of marrying for love seems to make irrelevant Tranio's elaborate disguise plots – one wonders why it took so long for elopement to present itself as an answer. Abduction, however, only becomes a possibility once Baptista decides to seal the assurance away from home. Baptista opens the play by shutting himself and his youngest daughter within the walls of his home, locking her away from potential suitors (I.i.90–101). At the end of the fourth act, a marriage contract, as he thinks, in sight, he ventures beyond those walls, relaxes his vigilance, and so loses in an instant both his daughter and his investment.

Act IV, scene v

1–25 'I know it is the moon'

This scene marks the turning-point in the taming plot, and reprises the end of Act IV, scene iii where Katherina and Petruchio argue whether it is morning or afternoon. This time, however, insisting on his marital right to rename, and so recreate, his wife's reality, Petruchio literally calls day night, rhetorically framing the sun and moon as symbolic opposites. Hortensio's intervention at line 11 can seem in performance to reveal something about what motivates the decisive moment when the wife submits to her husband. Katherina and Petruchio quickly fall into what has become a familiar linguistic pattern, the emphatic parallelism and verbal repetition of their stichomythic exchange at lines 4–5 implying a well-matched set of wills, obstinately pulling in opposite directions. As at the end of IV.iii, Petruchio delivers a five-line speech that shows his power to end, or at least further delay, their trip to her father's house so long as Katherina 'cross[es]' his will.

This potential stand-off, however, is ended by a third-party intervention. Hortensio, the apprentice wife-tamer, provides in IV.iii and this scene an additional perspective on Petruchio's and Katherina's marital relations and – always assuming the character is not cut from these scenes in performance (see Chapter 4, pp. 120–7) – his response shapes an audience's perception of character and situation. Here, Hortensio may seem desperate or exasperated, he may try to intimidate Katherina, or he may even burst out laughing; he might seem, in other words, as relentless as Petruchio, or the first to break, and the actor's choice of delivery of his line will help to shape an audience's interpretation of Katherina's sudden change of attitude. Such nuances of performance are crucial, particularly in a scene that is open to widely divergent critical interpretation. When Katherina again falls into repetition and stichomythic dialogue at lines 16–18 to affirm, rather than contradict, Petruchio's opinion, is she giving up in defeat, taking pity on Hortensio, mocking her husband's madness, or something else entirely?

Scholarly and theatrical approaches to the taming plot are dominated by three distinct readings of Katherina's notorious final monologue (V.ii.135–78), a speech on marriage and obedience which finds its beginning in this sudden *volte-face* in the sun–moon scene. The first view is that Katherina's submission is entirely ironic and that Petruchio, the gull, triumphantly takes as duty what is merely a feigned deference to his will; the second line, more grim, is that Katherina's spirit is brutally and conclusively beaten down by Petruchio's taming methods; and the third is that Katherina willingly and happily enters into a theatrical game, initiated by Petruchio, that unites the two of them, the play's 'mad-brained' outsiders, in a creative space able to free them both from oppressive social constrictions (these critical and theatrical interpretations are discussed further in Chapters 4 and 6). Textual support can be cited for any of these views, and spectators are guided in performance one way or another through such extra-textual prompts as body language, tone of voice, sound effects and music cues, lighting design, and the apparent reactions of an onstage participant and witness to the taming such as Hortensio.

26–76   'My name is called Vincentio'

The sudden and unexpected introduction of the real Vincentio creates a moment of powerful dramatic irony as the audience, but none of the onstage characters, realizes the potential problems his arrival in Padua will cause for Tranio, Lucentio, Biondello and Bianca. Petruchio's response, however – to welcome Vincentio as a father, and tell him that his son has married Bianca – is confusing. Is he referring to the real Lucentio, or to Tranio in disguise as Lucentio? Either way, how could Petruchio, in Verona, know of Bianca's marriage in Padua? Moreover, why does Hortensio confirm the news? He is not privy to the disguise plot, and only knows the false Lucentio has renounced Bianca as unfaithful (IV.ii.22–34). There is a glitch in the plot that a quick spectator might notice, and that a company might choose to rectify in performance through cuts, revision or stage business. For example, in a 2003 Stratford, Ontario, production, the sudden arrival of a letter by Pony Express self-consciously drew attention to, and resolved, the issue of how Petruchio gets his information.

However, what seems most strange about the problem is the way Petruchio and Vincentio dwell for fully seventeen lines on a marriage Petruchio, within the fiction of the play, can know nothing about. In error though it is, the precipitate marriage announcement provides opportunity briefly to slow the pace and drive home the point that this new character is the *real* Vincentio, Lucentio's *real* father. Shakespeare, in other words, is perhaps less concerned about those overly attentive spectators who manage to spot a small logical inconsistency as the action flows past, than about spectators whose attention might be flagging at the end of a busy fourth act. Presumably likewise worried about losing his audience in this new development, Monette further emphasized the coincidence of their encounter by having Grumio and Hortensio, listening to the conversation, shout 'Aah!' in response to each new revelation.

77–9   'Have to my widow!'

In the final scene of *A Shrew*, Sly awakens to find the lord gone and himself once again transformed into a tinker. Thinking that the play was a dream, he resolves to go home and tame his own wife (see Chapter 3, p. 110). This epilogue has proven of immense use in the theatre, where it is frequently integrated into Shakespeare's play to distance further from the audience's reality the misogynist content of the taming plot. The play within a play, already a staged fiction, is transformed into a dream, the ludicrous and/or pathetic fantasy world of a socially disempowered male (see Chapter 4, pp. 137–9). Although the epilogue does not appear in *The Shrew*, the substance of Sly's commentary is transferred to this three-line soliloquy in which Hortensio (like Sly, a would-be pupil with a domineering wife) finds himself 'put . . . in heart' by Petruchio's example. Shakespeare thus sacrifices the overtly metatheatrical conclusion of *A Shrew* in order to allow his audience in the final scene to witness for themselves Hortensio's relationship with his 'froward' widow, and the (lack of) success with which he has been able to put into effect his education at the taming-school.

ACT V

Act V, scene i

1–6   'I marvel Cambio comes not'

The Folio's 'Gremio is out before' is an unusual direction since, rather than merely getting Gremio onto the stage to deliver his lines, through the precision of its timing it sets up as a visual effect a moment of dramatic irony. Gremio's presence for the first five lines of the scene firmly situates this character within the well-established traditions of the *commedia* pantaloon, since he is hoodwinked by the young lovers and fails to see the elopement happening, literally, before his eyes. His single line (l. 6) confirms he still has not seen through Lucentio's disguise and emphasizes his gullibility.

Lucentio might marry Bianca and confront his father in his own likeness with the costume change transforming Cambio into Lucentio happening before the lovers enter the scene. A new set of clothes would add a visual pun to Bianca's explanation at l. 111 that 'Cambio' (the name translates from the Italian as 'I change') 'is changed into Lucentio'. But this costuming would equally imply that Baptista, out of keeping with the usual conventions of Shakespearean comedy – and *Shrew* in particular – manages to recognize the man he thinks is his servant through the gentleman's clothing he is currently wearing. The decision about when to discard the disguise will vary from one performance to another, and there is no requirement for Lucentio to appear 'as himself', as editors often direct, at the beginning of this scene. Crucially, though, if Lucentio still looks like Cambio when the scene opens, then the lovers will have to seem to slip away out of sight of Gremio; if Lucentio appears as himself, it seems feasible that the lovers might walk across the stage in plain view of the other suitor, who fails to suspect the device.

7–98   'Lay hold on him'

The answer to the riddle of two Vincentios is instantly solved by Petruchio – one of them must be lying – but it proves less easy to identify which figure is the substitute. The actor playing Petruchio might direct his accusation of 'flat knavery' (ll. 31–3) to his travelling companion, to the father in the window, or in confusion to both. The irony of this moment is that the unravelling of the disguise plot depends on discerning names and matching them accurately to the things they are supposed to represent. The taming plot, by contrast, was brought to its resolution through exactly the opposite means – an agreement to call the sun anything Petruchio wills it to be.

The problems of identity suffered by Vincentio are therefore not dissimilar to the experiences of Katherina at Petruchio's hands. Tranio, Biondello and the Pedant, like Petruchio, use disciplining measures – rather than starve Vincentio and keep him without sleep, they threaten to send him to jail – to try to force Lucentio's father to submit to (if not accept as true) their idiosyncratic, and personally advantageous, construction of reality. In *A Shrew*, this is the only time Sly intervenes to alter the direction of the play within a play, insisting that 'we'll have no sending to prison, that's flat' (see Chapter 3, p. 108).

Tellingly, the juxtaposed plights of Vincentio and Katherina come to very different conclusions. Whereas Vincentio exits promising 'to be revenged for this villainy' (l. 124) and the perpetrators of the intended offence run away '*as fast as may be*' (l. 101), Katherina is forced, again, to demonstrate her continued obedience to Petruchio's word. The contrast provided by the parallel examples of father and wife suggests a few possible conclusions: that Vincentio overreacts to being 'haled and abused' (l. 97); that Katherina has been done a correspondingly gross injustice under which she continues to suffer; or, more generally and provocatively, that this early modern comedy implicitly assumes as one of its basic ideological premises the unequal rights and powers of men and women.

99–129　'I will in to be revenged'
The confusions of identity prompted by the disguise plot are resolved with Lucentio's revelation of his marriage to Bianca; however, the consequences of his deception are less easily managed. Specifically, the play's comic reconciliation – assuming it occurs at all – is deferred to the narrative and theatrical gap between V.i and V.ii, both fathers, for different reasons, responding with anger and/or dismay to Lucentio's explanation that 'Love wrought these miracles' (l. 112). A production that wished to present a straightforwardly comic ending, parents and children happily reunited, might cut lines 124–7 (or more). Otherwise, it might suggest through extra-textual business – the two fathers suddenly bursting into laughter, or kissing Lucentio and Bianca – that they have come to terms with the events that have occurred without their knowledge or permission. In *A Shrew*, Vincentio's anger at the elopement, and specifically with the discrepancies of degree between his son and Baptista's daughter, emerges as a major issue (see Chapter 3, p. 108).

130–41　'kiss me, Kate'
This scene replays Act I, scene i with a difference: whereas there it was Katherina who provided 'some show' and 'good pastime' for the

newcomers, here it is Lucentio and Tranio who provide the spectacle
for Katherina and Petruchio who 'stand aside' at l. 54 to 'see the end
of this controversy'. However, before they exit, Petruchio insists on
making a spectacle (of) himself by demanding a kiss of his wife 'in the
midst of the street' (l. 133). This is neither the first nor last time
Petruchio uses this alliterative construction to demand a kiss
(compare II.i.317 and V.ii.179), and each production will decide how,
and how often, an audience sees the two of them kiss. While a kiss is
fairly easy to avoid altogether at Act II.i (but Petruchio – or
Katherina? – may seem to insist), some kind of gesture seems likely
here in order to forestall a repetition of the stand-off that has plagued
from the beginning their journey to her father's house. However,
whether it is a highly eroticized encounter as in the Miller production
(see Chapter 4, p. 136), a chaste peck on the cheek as in the Zeffirelli
film, or something completely unexpected from the lines on the page
– a chocolate Hershey's kiss, for instance – can only be decided in
performance, as can the response of the few or many (assuming there
are any) onstage spectators.

Act V, scene ii

1–11   'welcome to my house'

A 'banquet' consisting of fruit, delicate and expensive confectionary,
and wine was the last course of a rich feast, and the guests would enjoy
it in another, more casual, room or building. This final scene therefore
picks up the story after the explanations have been made and Bianca's
impromptu wedding party is well under way. Shakespeare's comedies
conventionally end in multiple marriages, with the confusions of the
previous four acts finally resolved. The imagery of music and war in
the opening two lines of Lucentio's graciously phrased speech
balances against the guests' present friendship their earlier, discordant
positions, and he acknowledges their 'scapes and perils' (the lovers'
fraught ordeals, but also, potentially, their moral transgressions)
precisely in order to deny them space at the table. Paradoxically,
although the theme of his speech is harmony and closure – even the
banquet serves 'to close our stomachs up' – Lucentio's language of
reconciliation carries within it the idea of conflict.

Spectators, crucially, are not privy to the financial and legal negotiations that took place after the children's elopement, and so they
have to infer through the appearance and manner of the characters at
the banquet whether, for example, Vincentio 'content[ed]' Baptista
for the loss of his daughter, or 'slit [Tranio's] nose' in revenge for
trying to send him to jail (V.i.119–24). As a result, whether this party
seems a festive, tense, or even miserable affair will depend on how
the words on the page are nuanced in performance through such
non-verbal signals as the physical proximity of the fathers to each
other, and the warmth with which at lines 4–5 they seem to accept
their children's welcome.

12–34   'To her widow!'
This scene marks the first appearance of Hortensio's bride,
mentioned in dialogue as late as IV.ii.37–9, and again at IV.v.77–9.
Although she has married Hortensio, and so legally changed her
marital status from widow to wife, spectators continue to hear this
character named in dialogue as 'widow' (the only exception to this is
where Hortensio 'entreat[s his] wife' at V.ii.85). The effect of this
unusual designation is further reinforced for readers of the Folio,
who see all of her speeches and entries marked as either 'Widdow' or
'Wid'. Such textual and paratextual cues suggest strongly that she is
less character than character type. By embodying, even after
marriage, early modern cultural stereotypes about widows, this
figure offers a third example of female assertiveness and independence to set in contrast to the other brides.

35–62   'Have at you for a bitter jest or two'
Petruchio manages to draw into a variably bawdy and jibing wordplay almost all of the onstage characters, setting them in opposition
either to himself or each other. The fast-paced repartee and biting
humour might come across in performance as good-natured wit, but
the substance of the banter – Hortensio and Petruchio are cowed
husbands, Katherina a shrew, Gremio a cuckold, Tranio a failed lover
– is such that the 'jest[s]' (l. 45) could seem, rather, to draw blood.
Tellingly, the antagonistic cut and thrust of the dialogue is metaphorically figured as blood-fights (ll. 33–5), rutting animals locking horns

(ll. 39–41), and hunters after prey (ll. 46–51). In Miller's production, in order to make Bianca seem to take over the shrewish role Katherina has abandoned, careful manipulation of stage business and tone makes only Bianca's interjection come across as ill-humoured (see Chapter 4, p. 136).

63–114 'What's the wager?'

Money remains a key theme, shaping a perception of marriage as a contract and financial exchange. Here the negotiation of dowries and jointures, a process that hinges implicitly on the value of a woman to the men who bargain for her, is transformed into a crude economic competition and transaction, a wager, in which men bet on the relative merit of their wives as measured in terms of their evident obedience. As Petruchio implies at line 72, it was common practice in this period for men of degree and wealth to compete with, and test, each other's masculinity by wagering on the excellence of their hawks and hounds. The specific form the bet takes here figures a wife as another, perhaps even the most, valuable asset by means of which one man can assert primacy over his male peers.

To a large extent, then, the real issue in this scene is not the relations of power between wives and husbands, but honour among men. As a consequence, even if one or more of the three husbands were reluctant competitors, once proposed, the wager would be difficult to refuse without loss of face. It therefore makes a difference who comes up with the idea. In Shakespeare's play, it is Petruchio who initiates the wager; in A Shrew, the wager is set by the Lucentio figure, who taunts Katherine's husband into placing a bet. The moment could be played any number of ways in performance: Petruchio might seem bold and confident; he might seem stung by Baptista's words at lines 63–4 and recklessly propose a wager he knows he could lose; or a knowing look between Katherina and Petruchio when she finally enters might suggest they hatched the money-making plot between them before arriving at the banquet. The structural function of Hortensio's sudden marriage becomes clearly apparent as a sequence of refusals, one more abrupt than the former (Bianca cannot come; the widow will not come) allows suspense to build onstage and offstage in anticipation of Katherina's appearance.

115–34　'We will have no telling'

After winning the bet, saving his pride, and gaining from his father-in-law a second dowry, Petruchio insists on providing still further demonstration of his wife's obedience. What seems so remarkable about the sequence in which Katherina throws down her cap and delivers her long speech is how completely superfluous it is to the plot, seeming more like a bravado encore than a well-integrated part of the action. In productions such as that of Marowitz that stage Petruchio as an over-bearing bully, this action seems consistent with a project continually to test and display his wife's obedience. This episode, however, can prove problematic for productions that seek to emphasize a spirit of loving mutuality within marriage. Taylor cuts it from the banquet scene, opening instead with Katherina in the middle of her speech; Monette's Katherina looked searchingly at her husband before obeying his command (see Chapter 4, p. 141).

This perception of structural, and perhaps thematic, excess leads one to question its theatrical and/or interpretative purpose – what function is served by seeing a woman stamp on her cap, and hearing her enjoin to the others female subjection in marriage? This coda to the wager might allow Petruchio to revel in his wife's humiliation, showing off what he can make her do; it might be an extension of the taming process aimed at unruly wives on stage and in the theatre audience (Miller's Petruchio, for example, screams 'I say she shall!' to silence the recalcitrant widow); or it might represent the very means by which Katherina overthrows her subjection. Women were supposed to be silent and obedient, but by being forced to theatricalize her submission Katherina (and the actor who plays the part) might seem to subvert and implicitly reject that ideological position at the very moment she articulates it (on the metatheatricality of this speech, see Chapter 6, pp. 156–61).

135–44　'It blots thy beauty'

This entire speech is ostensibly addressed to the women onstage whom Katherina, on Petruchio's instruction, is lecturing on their duties to their husbands. These opening nine lines, with their injunction in the singular to 'unknit that threatening unkind brow', are often in performance directed specifically to a seemingly put-out

Widow, and only by extension to Bianca. Significantly, though, neither of these women speaks again. While it seems unlikely that in the earliest performances they would have exited the stage during Katherina's speech, it would be a powerful theatrical choice for modern production. This staging would upstage Katherina, leaving her to perform to a truncated – and exclusively male – onstage audience. Marowitz, like Taylor, cuts everything in the scene apart from the final speech. Staged as a tribunal, the unseen presence of anonymous female spectators is discerned only through their voices: the stage directions cue 'the unmistakeable murmur of women's voices; chatting, gossiping, conniving'. As the trial begins, '[t]he whispering stops' (see Chapter 4, p. 130).

145–53 'commits his body / To painful labour'

Katherina's parallel speech in *A Shrew* cites original sin and Eve's creation from the rib of Adam as sufficient reason for woman's utter subjugation to man (see Chapter 3, pp. 109–10). However, Shakespeare's version takes a very different emphasis, detailing not just a wife's obligations within marriage, but also the duty of a husband to support and protect a subordinate, and so dependent, family. Women do not, therefore, simply give, but also receive. This sense of reciprocal duty informs critical perspectives that find in the play a coherent, even progressive, theory of marriage (see Chapter 6, pp. 147–53). The effect is sometimes pointed in performance by Katherina turning her attention from her unruly female companions to her husband, who can seem suddenly and comically discomfited. Monette, who played the speech in large part as Katherina's love letter to her husband, at this moment chose to focus attention on a daughter's gratitude, Katherina crossing the stage to lay her hands on her father's shoulders (see Chapter 4, p. 141).

154–63 'a foul, contending rebel'

Katherina, by this point, has delivered nearly twenty lines of verse, chastising the women for their frowns and telling them why they have an obligation to obey their husbands. The speech could feasibly end here, and some productions have Petruchio, either assuming his wife is finished or trying to reassert a dominant place in the scene, try to interrupt her. This can thus become a powerful moment for Katherina as she continues to command centre stage, refusing to defer to her husband's voice. The potential for irony in such a presentation begins to surface, as Katherina's language of subordination can come to seem excessive, more than the occasion – or Petruchio – requires. Tellingly, Garrick sliced this speech into three short speeches, and gave some of the lines (and so the last word) to Petruchio, thus shifting the focus away from Katherina (see Chapter 4, p. 123).

'A Homily against Disobedience and Wilful Rebellion', a government authorized sermon read out in churches in the reign of Elizabeth I, draws explicit parallels between the relation of a wife to her husband and that of a subject to his or her king (see Chapter 3, pp. 110–12). This section of Katherina's speech asserts male power within marriage by drawing on the same analogy between household and state. Significantly, however, conduct books and sermons from the period sought to limit a husband's power and so prevent men from abusing their supposedly God-given position of authority within the household by advocating a moral concept of affective mutuality (see Chapter 3). Some productions draw out this sense of give and take within marriage by having Katherina heavily emphasize a wife's due obedience to her husband's '*honest* will' (see Chapter 4, p. 141).

Despite such possible inflections, this hierarchical relation between husband and wife can seem contentious from a modern perspective, even antagonistic. The neat analogy between structures of power within household and state entirely overlooks single-parent families and same-sex relationships, while Katherina's earlier description of a husband's 'painful labour' implicitly decries the potential for female leadership, or even participation, in the workplace. Clearly, this is another world from that familiar to most modern spectators. It still touches a nerve, however, because male–female relations – if not the precise social circumstances and ideological assumptions Katherina articulates – remain subjects of debate. Her polemic continues to seem relevant, rather than some obscure sixteenth-century issue, precisely because the frame of reference spectators and readers bring to this play is inevitably shaped by their own political stance on current male–female relations.

Especially in performance, the issues of gender and sexuality addressed by this play will not – and cannot – remain safely bounded off as purely 'historical' (see Chapter 6, pp. 154–6, and also Chapter 4, pp. 131–3 for Miller's treatment of history and politics).

164–74　'our lances are but straws'

Critical and theatrical approaches to this speech, as in the sun–moon scene, tend either to affirm Katherina's polemic as the positive expression of a position of shared, albeit different, responsibilities within marriage, or to reject it by suggesting that her words, the product of a systematic process of male brutality, are not her own (see Chapter 6, pp. 152–3 and Chapter 4, pp. 127–31). A possible way out of this dichotomy, a strategy commonly seen in performance, is through irony – to signal to the audience (through a wink, an exaggerated tone, or otherwise) that although Katherina's words may be her husband's, her spirit remains her own. The rhetoric of this passage, in particular, lends itself to such an interpretation since it seems to imply that women must be obedient only because they lack the means to rebel (see Chapter 6, pp. 157–8).

175–8　'My hand is ready'

Katherina's gesture of humility alludes to a pre-Reformation marriage ritual that may have survived in the memories of at least some of Shakespeare's earliest spectators. This ceremony required the bride to place her hand under her groom's foot to symbolize their hierarchical relation in marriage. The question for performance is whether the offer seems merely a rhetorical flourish. Katherina might hold out her hand, or conversely she may actually bend down as though in fact to place her hand beneath Petruchio's foot. If a production seeks to play up a sense of her speech as excessive, this latter movement could seem to top an already exaggerated delivery. Petruchio's response to any gesture she makes is crucial. He might seem brutal, expecting her to carry out the action, or he might at some key moment kneel down with her, symbolically raising her up as his equal. How one interprets the cruelty or mutuality within this particular marriage will be heavily influenced by this closing tableau.

179–88 'Come, Kate, we'll to bed'

After Petruchio's strong closing speech, framed in rhyming couplets, the Folio prints the stage direction '*Exit Petruchio*'. Stage directions in early modern drama, especially by the standards of modern readers, can seem incomplete or in error (see Chapter 1, pp. 10–11), and modern editors usually change this direction to read '*Exeunt Petruchio and Katherina*'. The unemended Folio cue, however, might prompt some provocative stagings, either in the theatre or in a reader's imagination. For instance, it remains unclear from the dialogue whether Petruchio and Katherina have yet consummated their marriage. Petruchio promises to keep his wife up all night after their arrival in Verona (IV.i.184–93), and while his methods of 'kill[ing] a wife with kindness' seem an unlikely context in which to have sex, a vow not to sleep does not preclude it. However, stage business such as cheers and hoots from the wedding guests often suggests that the culmination of Katherina's 'taming' as they exit together at the end of Act V is full sexual knowledge of her husband.

Significantly, though, if one follows the Folio direction and has Petruchio exit alone, the play might end very differently, with Katherina finishing her *tour de force* monologue only to continue to 'hold [her husband] at bay' (V.ii.56). The issue, finally, is whether a production wishes to stage a solid, and conventionally comic, presentation of marital harmony and sexual fulfilment, or whether critically and theatrically it seems preferable to suggest a more qualified resolution (see Chapter 4, p. 136 for Miller's decision to end the production with the assembled group singing a Puritan hymn).

3 The Play's Sources and Cultural Context

The following extracts suggest some of the literary and cultural contexts within which *The Taming of the Shrew* found life in performance. The first three offer sources and analogues for the three separate strands of Shakespeare's play: the disguise plot, the taming plot, and the Sly material. The next four passages are taken from sixteenth- and seventeenth-century sermons, treatises and pamphlets. These extracts offer contrasting perspectives on women's legal and moral rights within marriage as well as documenting various abuses of the institution.

Gascoigne's *Supposes* (1566)

George Gascoigne published *Supposes* in 1566, a translation of Ariosto's 1509 Italian comedy *I Suppositi*. This play provided Shakespeare with the substance of the disguise plot surrounding Bianca and her multiple suitors. In *Supposes*, the only rivals for the daughter's love are the young nobleman in disguise as a servant, his servant in disguise as his master, and the wealthy pantaloon. Shakespeare weaves into this story another suitor (Hortensio), a second daughter (Katherina), a husband for her (Petruchio), and a taming story loosely based on English ballad traditions.

This extract is from the second edition of *Supposes* (1587). This scene was reworked as two separate episodes in *Taming of the Shrew*: the bargaining scene in which Tranio (in disguise as Lucentio) offers a false jointure in order to win Bianca in marriage, conditional on his father's approval of the terms (II.i.325–404), and the encounter with the traveller who will play the false father (IV.ii.59–121). The servant who corresponds to Shakespeare's Tranio is named 'Dulipo', and his master 'Erostrato' (this character, like Lucentio, is in disguise as a servant).

EROSTRATO: What news?

DULIPO: Good.

EROSTRATO: Indeed?

DULIPO: Yea, excellent, we have as good as won the wager.

EROSTRATO: O how happy were I if this were true!

DULIPO: Hear you me. Yesternight in the evening I walked out and found Pasiphilo, and with small entreating I had him home to supper, where by such means as I used, he became my great friend, and told me the whole order of our adversary's determination. Yea, and what Damon [the Baptista father figure] doth intend to do also, and hath promised me that from time to time, what he can espy he will bring me word of it.

EROSTRATO: I cannot tell whether you know him or no, he is not to trust unto, a very flattering and a lying knave.

DULIPO: I know him very well, he cannot deceive me, and this that he hath told me I know must needs be true.

EROSTRATO: And what was it in effect?

DULIPO: That Damon had purposed to give his daughter in marriage to this doctor, on the dower that he hath proffered.

EROSTRATO: Are these your good news? Your excellent news?

DULIPO: Stay a while, you will understand me before you hear me.

EROSTRATO: Well, say on.

DULIPO: I answered to that, I was ready to make her the like dower.

EROSTRATO: Well said.

DULIPO: Abide, you hear not the worst yet.

EROSTRATO: O God, is there any worse behind?

DULIPO: Worse? Why, what assurance could you suppose that I might make without some special consent from Philogano, my father?

EROSTRATO: Nay, you can tell, you are better scholar than I.

DULIPO: Indeed, you have lost your time, for the books that you toss nowadays treat of small science.

EROSTRATO: Leave thy jesting, and proceed.

DULIPO: I said further, that I received letters lately from my father, whereby I understood that he would be here very shortly to perform all that I had proffered. Therefore I required him to request Damon on my behalf that he would stay his promise to the doctor for a fortnight or more.

EROSTRATO: This is somewhat yet, for by this means I shall be sure to linger and live in hope one fortnight longer, but at the fortnight's end when Philogano cometh not, how shall I then do? Yea, and though he came, how may I any way hope of his consent, when he shall see that to follow this amorous enterprise I have set aside all study, all remembrance of my duty, and all dread of shame. Alas, alas, I may go hang myself.

DULIPO: Comfort yourself, man, and trust in me. There is a salve for every sore, and doubt you not, to this mischief we shall find a remedy.

EROSTRATO: O friend, revive me, that hitherto since I first attempted this matter have been continually dying.

DULIPO: Well, hearken a while then. This morning I took my horse and rode into the fields to solace myself, and as I passed the ford beyond St. Anthony's gate, I met at the foot of the hill a gentleman riding with two or three men, and as methought by his habit and his looks, he should be none of the wisest. He saluted me, and I him. I asked him from whence he came, and whither he would? He answered that he had come from Venice, then from Padua, now was going to Ferrara, and so to his country, which is Sienna. As soon as I knew him to be a Siennese, suddenly lifting up mine eyes (as it were with an admiration), I said unto him, 'Are you a Siennese, and come to Ferrara?' 'Why not,' said he. Quoth I, half and more with a trembling voice, 'Know you the danger that should ensue if you be known in Ferrara to be a Siennese?' He, more than half amazed, desired me earnestly to tell him what I meant.

EROSTRATO: I understand not whereto this tendeth.

DULIPO: I believe you – but hearken to me.

EROSTRATO: Go to then.

DULIPO: I answered him in this sort, 'Gentleman, because I have heretofore found very courteous entertainment in your country, being a student there, I account myself as it were bound to a Siennese, and therefore if I knew of any mishap towards any of that country, God forbid but I should disclose it. And I marvel that you knew not of the injury that your countrymen offered this other day to the ambassadors of Count Hercules.'

EROSTRATO: What tales he telleth me. What appertain these to me?

DULIPO: If you will hearken awhile, you shall find them no tales, but that they appertain to you more than you think for.

EROSTRATO: Forth.

DULIPO: I told him further, 'These ambassadors of Count Hercules had divers mules, wagons, and charets [carts], laden with divers costly jewels, gorgeous furniture, and other things which they carried as presents passing that way to the King of Naples, the which were not only stayed in Sienna by the officers whom you call customers, but searched, ransacked, tossed and turned, and in the end exacted for tribute, as if they had been the goods of a mean merchant.'

EROSTRATO: Whither the devil will he? Is it possible that this gear appertain anything to my cause? I find neither head nor foot in it.

DULIPO: O how impatient you are. I pray you stay a while.

EROSTRATO: Go to yet awhile then.

DULIPO: I proceeded, that upon these causes the Duke sent his Chancellor to declare the case unto the Senate there, of whom he had the most uncourteous answer that ever was heard. Whereupon he was so enraged with all of that country that for revenge he had sworn to spoil as many of them as ever should come to Ferrara, and to send them home in their doublet and their hose.

EROSTRATO: And I pray thee how couldest thou upon the sudden devise or imagine such a lie? And to what purpose?

DULIPO: You shall hear by and by a thing as fit for our purpose, as any could have happened.

EROSTRATO: I would fain hear you conclude.

DULIPO: You would fain leap over the stile before you come at the hedge. I would you had heard me, and seen the gestures that I enforced to make him believe this.

EROSTRATO: I believe you, for I know you can counterfeit well.

DULIPO: Further I said, the Duke had charged upon great penalties that the inn-holders and victuallers should bring word daily of as many Siennese as came to their houses. The gentleman being (as I guessed at the time) a man of small *sapientia* [wisdom], when he heard these news, would have turned his horse another way.

EROSTRATO: By likelihood he was not very wise when he would believe that of his country, which if it had been true every man must needs have known it.

DULIPO: Why not? When he had not been in his country for a month past, and I told him this had happened within these seven days.

EROSTRATO: Belike he was of small experience.

DULIPO: I think of as little as may be, but best of all for our purpose, and good adventure it was that I met with such a one. Now hearken, I pray you.

EROSTRATO: Make an end, I pray thee.

DULIPO: He, as I say, when he heard these words, would have turned the bridle. And I feigning a countenance as though I were somewhat pensive and careful for him, paused awhile, and after with a great sigh said to him, 'Gentleman, for the courtesy that, as I said, I have found in your country, and because your affairs shall be the better dispatched, I will find the means to lodge you in my house. And you shall say to every man that you are a Sicilian of Cathanea, your name Philogano, father to me that am indeed of that country and city, called here Erostrato. And I, to pleasure you, will during your abode here do you reverence as you were my father.'

EROSTRATO: Out upon me! What a gross-headed fool am I! Now I perceive whereto this tale tendeth.

DULIPO: Well, and how like you of it?

EROSTRATO: Indifferently. But one thing I doubt.

DULIPO: What is that?

EROSTRATO: Marry, that when he hath been here two or three days, he shall hear of every man that there is no such thing between the Duke and the town of Sienna.

DULIPO: As for that, let me alone. I do entertain and will entertain him so well, that within these two or three days I will disclose unto him all the whole matter, and doubt not but to bring him in for performance of as much as I have promised to Damon. For what hurt can it be to him, when he shall bind a strange name and not his own?

EROSTRATO: What, think you he will be entreated to stand bound for a dower of two thousand ducats by the year?

DULIPO: Yea, why not if it were ten thousand, as long as he is not indeed the man that is bound?

EROSTRATO: Well, if it be so, what shall we be the nearer to our purpose?

DULIPO: Why, when we have done as much as we can, how can we do any more?

EROSTRATO: And where have you left him?

DULIPO: At the inn, because of his horses. He and his man shall lie in my house.

EROSTRATO: Why brought you him not with you?

DULIPO: I thought better to use your advice first.

EROSTRATO: Well, go take him home, make him all the cheer you can, spare for no cost, I will allow it.

DULIPO: Content. Look where he cometh.

EROSTRATO: Is this he? Go meet him. By my troth he looks even like a
good soul. He that fisheth for him might be sure to catch a cod's head.
I will rest here awhile to decipher him.

'A Merry Jest of a Shrewd and Curst Wife' (*c.* 1550)

The story of a husband who tames his unruly wife survives in more
than 400 English ballads, folktales, poems and plays. This one, 'A
Merry Jest of a Shrewd and Curst Wife Lapped in Morel's Skin, for
Her Good Behaviour' (first published around 1550), is frequently cited
as particularly relevant to *The Taming of the Shrew*. It contrasts a
younger, obedient daughter to an elder, belligerent daughter, and
ends with the wife staging her new-learned obedience in front of her
incredulous family. This extract reprints the final lines of the poem
from the second edition of 1580 (sigs. E3–G1^v).

> How the goodman caused Morel to be slain, and the hide salted, to lay
> his wife therein to sleep.

'Now will I begin my wife to tame,
That all the world shall it know.
I would be loath her for to shame,
Though she do not care, you may me trow.
Yet will I her honesty regard,
And it preserve, wherever ye may.
But Morel that is in yonder yard
His hide therefore he must leese [lose], in fay.'

And so he commanded anon
To slay old Morel, his great horse,
And flay him then, the skin from the bone,
To wrap it about his wife's white corse.
Also he commanded of a birchen tree
Rods to be made a good great heap;
And sware by dear God in Trinity,
His wife in his cellar should skip and leap.

'The hide must be salted,' then he said eke,
'Because I would not have it stink.
I hope herewith she will be meek,
For this I trow will make her shrink.
And bow at my pleasure, when I her bid,
And obey my commandments both loud and still.
Or else I will make her body bleed,
And with sharp rods beat her my fill.'

[. . .]

How the curst wife in Morel's skin lay,
Because she would not her husband obey.

'Now will I my sweet wife trim
According as she deserveth to me.
I swear by God and by Saint Sim,
With birchen rods well beat shall she be.
And after that in Morel's salt skin
I will her lay and full fast bind,
That all her friends and eke her kin
Shall her long seek or [ere] they her find.'

Then he her met, and to her gan say,
'How sayest thou, wife, wilt thou be master yet?'
She sware by God's body, and by that day,
And suddenly with her fist she did him hit,
And defied him, 'drivel' [imbecile] at every word,
Saying, 'Precious whoreson, what dost thou think?
I set not by thee a stinking turd.
Thou shalt get of me neither meat nor drink.'

'Sayest thou me that, wife?' quoth he then.
With that, in his arms he gan her catch.
Straight to the cellar with her he ran,
And fastened the door with lock and latch,
And threw the key down him beside,
Asking her then if she would obey.
Then she said, 'Nay, for all thy pride,'
But she was master, and would abide alway.

'Then,' quoth he, 'we must make a fray.'
And with that her clothes he gan to tear.
'Out upon thee, whoreson!' then she did say.
'Wilt thou rob me of all my gear?
It cost thee naught, thou arrant thief.'
And quickly she got him by the head.
With that she said, 'God give thee a mischief,
And them that fed thee first with bread.'

They wrestled together thus, they two,
So long that the clothes asunder went,
And to the ground he threw her tho [then],
That clean from the back her smock he rent.
In every hand, a rod he got,
And laid upon her a right good pace,
Asking of her, 'What game was that?'
And she cried out, 'Whoreson, alas! alas!

'What wilt thou do? Wilt thou kill me?
I have made thee a man of naught.
Thou shalt repent it, by God's pity,
That ever this deed thou hast ywrought.'
'I care not for that, dame,' he did say,
'Thou shalt give over, or [ere] we depart,
The mastership all, or all this day
I will not cease to make thee smart.'

Ever he laid on, and ever she did cry,
'Alas! Alas that ever I was born!
Out upon thee, murderer, I thee defy,
Thou hast my white skin, and my body all to-torn.
Leave off betime, I counsel thee.'
'Nay, by God, dame, I say not so yet.
I swear to thee, by Mary so free,
We begin but now – this is the first fit.

'Once again we must dance about,
And then thou shalt rest in Morel's skin.'
He gave her then so many a great clout,
That on the ground the blood was seen.

Within a while, he cried, 'New rods, new!'
With that she cried full loud, 'Alas!'
'Dance yet about, dame, thou came not where it grew.'
And suddenly with that in a swoon she was.

He spied that, and up he her hent,
And wrang her hard then by the nose.
With her to Morel's skin straight he went,
And therein full fast he did her close.
Within a while she did revive,
Through the gross salt that did her smart.
She thought she should never have gone on live
Out of Morel's skin, so sore is her heart.

When she did spy that therein she lay,
Out of her wit she was full nigh,
And to her husband then did she say,
'How canst thou do this villainy?'
'Nay, how sayest thou, thou cursèd wife,
In this foul skin I will thee keep
During the time of all thy life,
Therein forever to wail and weep.'

With that her mood began to sink,
And said, 'Dear husband, for grace I call.
For I shall never sleep nor wink
Till I get your love, whatso befall.
And I will never to you offend,
In no manner of wise, of all my life,
Nor to do nothing that may pretend
To displease you with my wits five.

'For father nor mother, whatsoever they say,
I will not anger you, by God in throne,
But glad will your commandments obey,
In presence of people, and eke alone.'
'Well, on that condition thou shalt have
Grace, and fair bed to rest thy body in;
But if thou rage more, so God me save,
I will wrap thee again in Morel's skin.'

Then he took her out in his arms twain,
And beheld her so piteously with blood arrayed.
'How thinkest thou, wife, shall we again
Have such business more?' to her he said.
She answered, 'Nay, my husband dear,
While I you know, and you know me,
Your commandments I will, both far and near,
Fulfil alway in every degree.'

'Well then, I promise thee, by God, even now,
Between thee and me shall never be strife.
If thou to my commandments quickly bow,
I will thee cherish all the days of my life.'
In bed she was laid, and healèd full soon,
As fair and clear as she was beforn.
What he her bid was quickly done,
To be diligent, iwis, she took no scorn.

Then was he glad, and thought in his mind,
'Now have I done myself great good,
And her also, we shall it find,
Though I have shed part of her blood.
For as methink she will be meek,
Therefore I will her father and mother
Bid to guest now the next week,
And of our neighbours many other.'

How the goodman did bid her father and mother to guest, and many
    of his neighbours, that they might see his wife's patience.

Great pain he made his wife to take
Against the day that they should come.
Of them was none that there should lack,
I dare well say unto my doom.
Yea, father and mother, and neighbours all,
Did thither come to make good cheer.
Soon they were set in general;
The wife was diligent as did appear.

Father and mother was welcome then,
And so were they all, in good fay.

The husband sat there like a man;
The wife did serve them all that day.
The goodman commanded what he would have;
The wife was quick at hand.
'What now!' thought the mother, 'This arrant knave
Is master, as I understand.

'What may this mean,' then she gan think,
'That my daughter so diligent is?
Now can I neither eat nor drink,
Till I it know, by heaven bliss.'
When her daughter came again
To serve at the board, as her husband bade,
The mother stared with her eyen twain,
Even as one that had been mad.

All the folk that at the board sat
Did her behold then, everichone.
The mother from the board her got,
Following her daughter, and that anon,
And in the kitchen she her found,
Saying unto her in this wise,
'Daughter, thou shalt well understand,
I did not teach thee after this guise.'

'Ah, good mother! Ye say full well;
All things with me is not as ye ween.
If ye had been in Morel's fell
As well as I, it should be seen.'
'In Morel's fell! What devil is that?'
'Marry, mother, I will it you show,
But beware that you come not thereat,
Lest you yourself then do beshrew.

'Come down now in this cellar so deep,
And Morel's skin there shall you see,
With many a rod that hath made me to weep,
When the blood ran down fast by my knee.'
The mother this beheld, and cried out 'Alas!'
And ran out of the cellar as she had been wood.

She came to the table where the company was,
And said, 'Out, whoreson! I will see thy heart blood.'

'Peace, good mother! Or, so have I bliss,
Ye must dance else as did my wife,
And in Morel's skin lie that well salted is,
Which you should repent all the days of your life.'
All they that were there held with the young man,
And said he did well in every manner degree.
When dinner was done, they departed all then;
The mother no longer durst there be.

The father abode last, and was full glad,
And gave his children his blessing, iwis,
Saying the young man full well done had,
And merrily departed withouten miss.
This young man was glad ye may be sure
That he had brought his wife to this.
God give us all grace in rest to endure,
And hereafter to come unto his bliss.

Thus was Morel slain out of his skin
To charm a shrew, so have I bliss.
Forgive the young man, if he did sin,
But I think he did nothing amiss.
He did all thing even for the best,
As it well provèd then.
God save our wives from Morel's nest,
I pray you say all, amen.

Thus endeth the jest of Morel's skin,
Where the curst wife was lappèd in.
Because she was of a shrewd leer,
Thus was she served in this manner.

FINIS   Quoth Master Charm-her:
He that can charm a shrewd wife
     Better than thus,
Let him come to me, and fetch ten pound
     And a golden purse.

Sly Scenes from *The Taming of A Shrew* (1594)

The precise relationship between Shakespeare's comedy and the anonymous play *A Pleasant Conceited History, called The Taming of A Shrew* (1594) remains in doubt (see Chapter 1, pp. 1–5). Despite this uncertainty, the more extensive Sly passages in *A Shrew*, reprinted below, are frequently incorporated into theatrical productions of *The Shrew*. Also reprinted here as useful points of comparison between the two plays are the words of the Duke of Sestos (Shakespeare's Vincentio figure) upon discovery of his son's marriage, and Katherina's final-act monologue.

PASSAGE A: The placement of this passage has no precise equivalent in *The Taming of the Shrew*, but falls towards the middle or end of the second act. The 'fool' to whom Sly refers is Saunder, a character who corresponds to Petruchio's servant, Grumio, in *The Shrew*.

Then Sly speaks.

SLY: Sim, when will the fool come again?

LORD: He'll come again, my Lord, anon.

SLY: Gi's some more drink here. Souns, where's the tapster? Here, Sim, eat some of these things.

LORD: So I do, my Lord.

SLY: Here, Sim, I drink to thee.

Lord: My Lord, here comes the players again.

Sly: O brave, here's two fine gentlewomen.

*   *   *

PASSAGE B: This short exchange falls at V.i.6, after Lucentio and Bianca exit to be married, and as Petruchio, Kate, Vincentio and Grumio enter.

SLY: Sim, must they be married now?

LORD: Ay, my Lord.

Enter Ferando and Kate and Saunder.

SLY: Look, Sim, the fool is come again now.

*   *   *

PASSAGE C: This exchange might best be inserted at V.i.98. In *A Shrew* it falls after the Lucentio figure begs pardon of his father, the Duke of Sestos. His father threatens to send the false son and false father to jail. The Duke's speech following Sly's interjection is also reprinted.

Then Sly speaks.

SLY: I say we'll have no sending to prison.

LORD: My Lord, this is but the play; they're but in jest.

SLY: I tell thee, Sim, we'll have no sending to prison, that's flat. Why, Sim, am not I Don Christo Vary? Therefore I say they shall not go to prison.

LORD: No more they shall not, my Lord – they be run away.

SLY: Are they run away, Sim? That's well; then gi's some more drink and let them play again.

LORD: Here, my Lord.

Sly drinks and then falls asleep.

DUKE OF SESTOS:

Ah, treacherous boy that durst presume
To wed thyself without thy father's leave,
I swear by fair Cynthia's burning rays,
By Merops' head and by seven-mouthèd Nile,
Had I but known ere thou had'st wedded her,
Were in thy breast the world's immortal soul,
This angry sword should rip thy hateful chest,
And hewed thee smaller than the Lybian sands.
Turn hence thy face, O cruel, impious boy.
Alfonso, I did not think you would presume
To match your daughter with my princely house,
And ne'er make me acquainted with the cause.

*   *   *

PASSAGE D: This exchange falls between scenes i and ii of Act V.

Sly sleeps.

LORD:

Who's within there? Come hither, sirs. My Lord's
Asleep again. Go take him easily up,

And put him in his own apparel again,
And lay him in the place where we did find him,
Just underneath the alehouse side below,
But see you wake him not in any case.
BOY: It shall be done, my Lord. Come, help to bear him hence.

Exit Boy and servants, carrying Sly.

* * *

PASSAGE E: Katherina's speech (V.ii.135–78).

Then you that live thus by your pampered wills,
Now list to me and mark what I shall say.
Th'eternal power that, with his only breath,
Shall cause this end and this beginning frame,
Not in time, nor before time, but with time confused,
For all the course of years, of ages, months,
Of seasons temperate, of days and hours,
Are tuned and stopped by measure of his hand.
The first world was a form without a form,
A heap confused, a mixture all deformed,
A gulf of gulfs, a body bodiless,
Where all the elements were orderless
Before the great commander of the world,
The King of kings, the glorious God of heaven,
Who in six days did frame his heavenly work,
And made all things to stand in perfect course.
Then to his image he did make a man,
Old Adam, and from his side asleep,
A rib was taken, of which the Lord did make
The woe of man, so termed by Adam then,
Woman, for that by her came sin to us,
And for her sin was Adam doomed to die.
As Sarah to her husband, so should we:
Obey them, love them, keep and nourish them,
If they by any means do want our helps,
Laying our hands under their feet to tread,
If that by that we might procure their ease.
And for a precedent I'll first begin,

And lay my hand under my husband's feet.
She lays her hand under her husband's feet.

* * *

PASSAGE F: This exchange occurs at the very end of the action, after the completion of the play within a play.

> *Then enter two bearing of Sly in his own apparel again, and leaves him where they found him, and then goes out. Then enter the tapster.*
>
> TAPSTER:
> Now that the darksome night is overpassed,
> And dawning day appears in crystal sky,
> Now must I haste abroad. But soft, who's this?
> What, Sly? Oh, wondrous! Hath he lain here all night? I'll wake him. I think he's starved by this, but that his belly was so stuffed with ale. What, how, Sly! Awake, for shame!
>
> SLY: Sim, gi's some more wine. What's all the players gone? Am not I a lord?
>
> TAPSTER: A lord with a murrain. Come, art thou drunken still?
>
> SLY: Who's this? Tapster, O Lord sirrah, I have had the bravest dream tonight that ever thou heardest in all thy life.
>
> TAPSTER: Ay, marry, but you had best get you home, for your wife will course you for dreaming here tonight.
>
> SLY: Will she? I know now how to tame a shrew. I dreamt upon it all this night till now, and thou hast waked me out of the best dream that ever I had in my life. But I'll to my wife presently and tame her, too, and if she anger me.
>
> TAPSTER: Nay, tarry, Sly, for I'll go home with thee and hear the rest that thou hast dreamt tonight.
>
> *Exeunt omnes.*

'A Homily against Disobedience and Wilful Rebellion'

This sermon was delivered in Elizabethan churches at regular intervals throughout the calendar year. It outlines the absolute duty and obedience a subject owes to his or her prince, God's appointed minister on earth. The homily offers insight into Shakespeare's play in the way it likens the power of the husband over his household to the unquestioned authority of the prince over his subjects.

From *Certain Sermons or Homilies Appointed to be Read in Churches in the Time of Queen Elizabeth I*, 1570 (sigs. A2–B3)

[God] not only ordained that in families and households the wife should be obedient unto her husband, the children unto their parents, the servants unto their masters, but also, when mankind increased and spread itself more largely over the world, he by his holy word did constitute and ordain in cities and countries several and special governors and rulers, unto whom the residue of his people should be obedient . . .

But here let us rehearse two special places out of the New Testament which may stand in stead of all other. The first out of St. Paul's Epistle to the Romans and the thirteenth chapter [Romans 13:1–2], where he writeth thus unto all subjects, 'Let every soul be subject unto the higher powers, for there is no power but of God, and the powers that be are ordained of God. Whosoever therefore resisteth the power, resisteth the ordinance of God, and they that resist, shall receive to themselves damnation' . . . The second place is in St. Peter's first epistle and the second chapter [1 Peter 2:13–18], whose words are these, 'Submit yourselves unto all manner ordinance of man for the Lord's sake, whether it be unto the king, as unto the chief head, either [or] unto rulers, as unto them that are sent of him [the king] for the punishment of evil doers, but for the cherishing of them that do well. . . . Honour all men, love brotherly fellowship, fear God, honour the king. Servants, obey your masters with fear, not only if they be good and courteous, but also though they be froward.' Thus far out of St. Peter.

By these two places of the holy scriptures it is most evident that kings, queens, and other princes (for he speaketh of authority and power, be it in men or women) are ordained of God, are to be obeyed and honoured of their subjects; that such subjects as are disobedient or rebellious against their princes, disobey God, and procure their own damnation; that the government of princes is a great blessing of God, given for the commonwealth, specially of the good and godly, for the comfort and cherishing of whom God giveth and setteth up princes, and on the contrary part, to the fear and for the punishment of the evil and wicked. Finally, that if servants ought to obey their masters, not only being gentle but such as be froward, as well and much more ought subjects to be obedient, not only to their good and courteous, but also to their sharp and rigorous, princes. . . .

What shall subjects do then? Shall they obey valiant, stout, wise, and good princes, and contemn [despise], disobey, and rebel against children being their princes, or against undiscreet and evil governors? God forbid. For first, what a perilous thing were it to commit unto the subjects the judgement which prince is wise and godly, and his government good, and which is otherwise, as though the foot must judge of the head, an enterprise very heinous, and must needs breed rebellion. For who else be they that are most inclined to rebellion, but such haughty spirits? From whom springeth such foul ruin of realms? Is not rebellion the greatest of all mischiefs? And who are most ready to the greatest mischiefs, but the worst men? Rebels therefore, the worst of all subjects, are most ready to rebellion, as being the worst of all vices, and furthest from the duty of a good subject. As on the contrary part, the best subjects are most firm and constant in obedience, as in the special and peculiar virtue of good subjects . . .

But what if the prince be undiscreet and evil, indeed, and it also evident to all men's eyes, that he so is? I ask again, what if it be long [because] of the wickedness of the subjects that the prince is undiscreet or evil? Shall the subjects both by their wickedness provoke God, for their deserved punishment, to give them an undiscreet or evil prince, and also rebel against him and withal against God, who for the punishment of their sins did give them such a prince? . . . Nay, let us either deserve to have a good prince, or let us patiently suffer and obey such as we deserve. And whether the prince be good or evil, let us according to the counsel of the holy scriptures pray for the prince, for his continuance and increase in goodness, if he be good, and for his amendment if he be evil.

The Law's Resolutions of Women's Rights (1632)

This advice book, written by 'T.E.', is subtitled *The Law's Provision for Women* and carries on each page the running-title 'The Woman's Lawyer'. It sets out the legal rights and obligations of women before, during and after marriage (should she survive her husband). This extract is taken from Book 3, Chapters 7–9, and sets out the laws surrounding domestic violence and property ownership.

Section 7:   *The baron may beat his wife.*

[I]f a man beat an outlaw, a traitor, a pagan, his villein, or his wife it is dispunishable [not punishable], because by the law common these persons can have no action. God send gentlewomen better sport, or better company.

But it seemeth to be very true that there is some kind of castigation which law permits a husband to use, for if a woman be threatened by her husband to be beaten, mischieved [harmed], or slain, Fitzherbert sets down a writ which she may sue out of chancery to compel him to find surety of honest behaviour toward her, and that he shall neither do nor procure to be done to her (mark, I pray you) any bodily damage, otherwise than appertains to the office of a husband for lawful and reasonable correction . . . How far [such correction] extendeth I cannot tell.

Section 8:   *That which the husband hath is his own.*

But the prerogative of the husband is best discerned in his dominion over all extern things in which the wife, by combination [marriage], devesteth herself of propriety [property] in some sort, and casteth it upon her governor. For here practice everywhere agrees with the theoric of law, and forcing necessity submits women to the affection [condition] thereof: whatsoever the husband had before coverture either in goods or lands, it is absolutely his own, the wife hath therein no seisin at all. If anything when he is married be given him, he taketh it by himself distinctly to himself . . .

The very goods which a man giveth to his wife are still his own, her chain, her bracelets, her apparel, are all the goodman's goods. . . . A wife how gallant soever she be, glistereth but in the riches of her husband, as the moon hath no light, but it is the sun's. Yea, and her Phoebe borroweth sometime her own proper light from Phoebus.

Section 9:   *That which the wife hath is the husband's.*

For thus it is. If before marriage the woman were possessed of horses, neat [cattle], sheep, corn, wool, money, plate, and jewels, all manner of moveable substance is presently by conjunction the husband's, to sell, keep, or bequeath if he die. And though he bequeath them not, yet are they the husband's executor's and not the wife's which brought them to her husband.

Tell-Troth's New Year's Gift (1593)

This anonymous pamphlet provides a late-sixteenth century 'opinion piece' on the abuses of marriage. The first cause of marital problems the book identifies, reprinted here, is 'constrained love' (sigs. A3–A4ᵛ). A forced marriage, such as 'Tell-Troth' describes, is the fate Katherina endures, and Bianca narrowly avoids.

> The first cause [of jealousy], quoth he, is a constrained love, when as parents do by compulsion couple two bodies, neither respecting the joining of their hearts, nor having any care of the continuance of their welfare, but more regarding the linking of wealth and money together, than of love with honesty, will force affection without liking and cause love with jealousy. For either they marry their children in their infancy when they are not able to know what love is, or else match them with inequality, joining burning summer with key-cold winter, their daughters of twenty years old or under to rich cormorants of threescore or upwards. Whereby, either the dislike that likely grows with years of discretion engendereth disloyalty in the one, or the knowledge of the other's disability leads him to jealousy.
>
> What is the cause of so many household breaches, divorcements, and continual discontentments, but unnatural disagreements by unmutual contracts? . . . The man can provide for himself when the poor woman is void of all succour, and he will have a cloak to hide his misery when she shall want a cap to cover her extremity. She must bear the lumps and lours, if happily she escapes the blows, the biting words – if not worse, even cruel heart breakings and back-beatings. Thus shall the father's covetousness be cause of the child's undoing, and his heart's ease beginning of her woe and end of her happiness, his liking meeting with her loathing, which shall undo her by jealousy. . . . They do not match them with the mates their children's eyes have chosen, but with the men their own greedy desire have found out, little fore thinking of their children's after-grieving, and their own repenting. . . . They abhor and grow mad to hear their children entreat for the maids that please them, or for the men their souls love, but tyrant-like they say, *sic volo sic iubeo, stet pro ratione voluntas* – I like him, and thou shalt have him, love this man or I will loath thee. This effect hath covetousness in the father, and behold what discontentment it worketh in the child.
>
> He or she by duty is bound to their parents' commandment, and for

fear of their displeasure are linked to continual misery . . . he invents means to make her mourn, and leaves no practice untried which is like to procure her misery. They live in one house, as two enemies lie in the field, their habitation being severed, like two camps that be ready for battle. Havoc is made lavishly of that their fathers gathered corruptly, that either being spent lasciviously in the company of strangers, or licentiously in controversies at law. So great mischief ariseth of covetousness in matches of matrimony.

Henry Smith's *Preparative to Marriage* (1591)

Henry Smith was a popular sixteenth-century preacher. This extract, from one of his sermons (sigs. E1–F1ᵛ), outlines not just the duties of the wife to her husband, but those of the husband to his wife. It provides some sense of how women's disempowerment was tempered, at least from some pulpits, by a sense of shared, albeit unequal, responsibilities and obligations in marriage.

The man is to his wife in the place of Christ to his Church. Therefore, the Apostle requireth such an affection of him toward his spouse as Christ beareth toward his spouse . . . [The husband's] next duty to love is a fruit of his love; that is, to let all things be common between them which were private before. The man and wife are partners, like two oars in a boat; therefore, he must divide offices and affairs and goods with her, causing her to be feared and reverenced and obeyed of her children and servants like himself. For she is an under-officer in his commonweal, and therefore she must be assisted and borne out like his deputy, as the prince standeth with his magistrates for his own quiet, because they are the legs which bear him up . . . He may not say as husbands are wont to say, that which is thine is mine, and that which [is] mine is mine own, but that which is mine is thine and myself too . . .

Every wife is called goodwife. Therefore, if they be not good wives their names do belie them and they are not worth their titles, but answer to a wrong name, as players do upon a stage. This name pleaseth them well, but beside this a wife is called a yoke fellow, to show that she should help her husband to bear his yoke. That is, his grief must be her grief, and whether it be the yoke of poverty, or the yoke of envy, or the yoke of sickness, or the yoke of imprisonment, she must submit her neck to bear it patiently with him, or else she is not his yoke fellow, but his yoke, as though she were inflicted upon him for a penalty. . . . Besides a yoke fellow, she is called a helper, to help him in his business, to help him in his labours, to help him in his troubles, to help him in his sickness, like a woman physician, sometime with her strength, and sometime with her counsel. For sometime as God confoundeth the wise by the foolish, and the strong by the weak, so he teacheth the wise by the foolish, and helpeth the strong by the weak . . .

[S]he must not examine whether he be wise or simple, but that she is his wife, and therefore they which are bound must obey, as Abigail loved her husband though he were a fool. For the wife is as much despised for taking rule over her husband, as he for yielding it unto her. Therefore one saith that a mankind woman is a monster – that is, half a woman and half a man. It becomes not the mistress to be master, no more than it beseemeth the master to be mistress, but both to sail with their own wind. . . .

Though a woman be wise and painful, and have many good parts, yet if she be a shrew, her troublesome jarring in the end will make her honest behaviour unpleasant, as her over-pinching at last causeth her good housewifery to be evil spoken of. Therefore, although she be a wife, yet sometimes she must observe the servant's lesson, *not answering again*, and hold her peace to keep the peace. Therefore they which keep silence are well said to hold their peace, because silence oftentimes doth keep the peace, when words would break it.

4 Key Productions and Performances

[The Taming of the Shrew] *is, perhaps, the worst of all our great poet's productions. It is supposed to be presented before some great lord in his palace, and, by consequence, loses all power of imposing on the minds of an audience. It cannot for a moment pass for reality . . . Garrick, however, saw his way . . . [H]e had the judgement to select the most coherent scenes, and, without intermixing anything of his own, to let Shakespeare be the entire author of a very excellent comedy.*

> Arthur Murphy, Garrick biographer, 1801

[T]he last scene is altogether disgusting to modern sensibility. No man with any decency of feeling can sit it out in the company of a woman without being extremely ashamed of the lord-of-creation moral implied in the wager and the speech put into the woman's own mouth. Therefore the play, though still worthy of a complete and efficient representation, would need, even at that, some apology.

> George Bernard Shaw, 1897

There is, however, a larger question at stake than the merits or otherwise of this particular production. It is whether there is any reason to revive a play that seems totally offensive to our age and our society. My own feeling is that it should be put back firmly and squarely on the shelf.

> Michael Billington, theatre reviewer, 1979

Three theatre-goers, responding to different productions of *The Taming of the Shrew* and writing over a period of nearly two hundred years, seem to agree that Shakespeare's play is difficult to mount in performance. Murphy argues that it is badly written; Shaw and Billington, that its class and gender politics are unacceptable to modern audiences. Billington's 'larger question' is one worth pondering – if it poses such problems for spectators, why do we continue to stage this play at all? If one simply accepts that Shakespeare's comedies, *The Shrew* among them, will be staged, then the question is how one might address these perceived obstacles to enactment. Murphy favours abridgement, whereas Shaw prefers finding in performance some way to step aside from, or make amends for, the play's politics. This chapter considers how directors and actors, working in theatre and film, have handled in practice the interpretative challenges posed by this early Shakespearean comedy.

A perhaps surprising detail about the history of *The Shrew* in performance, especially in light of prevalent criticisms of the text as crude, offensive and ill-structured, is that it has long been – and continues to be – one of Shakespeare's most frequently staged plays. *Catharine and Petruchio*, a three-act afterpiece devised by David Garrick and first performed in 1754, commanded the British and American stages to the exclusion of the full-length script for fully ninety years. In this abbreviated and modified form, it proved to be 'the sixth most popular Shakespearean play on the stage from 1754 to 1800' (Haring-Smith, 1985, p. 15). More recently, *Shrew* ranks among the top ten plays produced at the Stratford Festival of Canada in the twenty-five years between 1978 and 2003, with more Festival Stage productions than either *King Lear* or *A Midsummer Night's Dream*. To turn to the other Stratford, Greg Doran calculates that it was the second most frequently produced play at the Royal Shakespeare Company in the sixteen years to 2003 (the year he directed it in the main house). Empirical evidence of its popularity is not limited to the theatre. In 1929, a feature-length film of *The Taming of the Shrew*, directed by Sam Taylor and starring Mary Pickford and Douglas Fairbanks, became the first play by Shakespeare to be filmed as a 'talkie', and since then, according to Diana E. Henderson (1997), '[m]ore than eighteen screen versions of the play have been produced in Europe and North America, putting *Shrew* in a select league with the "big four" tragedies [presumably *Hamlet*, *King Lear*, *Macbeth* and *Othello*], and outpacing those comedies scholars usually dub more "mature" ' (p. 148).

Paradoxically, then, rhetoric about the play's stylistic limitations and offensive content coexists with its continued reappearance on stage and screen. To look at this from an economic perspective, despite seeming with *The Merchant of Venice* a twentieth-century 'problem play' (Thompson, 1984, p. 21), *The Shrew* remains in performance a financially profitable theatrical investment. It therefore seems unlikely that dismay about its politics would, or in the present economic climate even could, lead many companies to follow Billington's call to put it back 'firmly and squarely' on the shelf.

Indeed, the play perhaps remains of interest to audiences, not despite, but because of, its controversial staging of a battle of the sexes, and there is some evidence to suggest that revivals of *The Shrew* tend to cluster around those decades when debates about 'the woman question' seem most pressing (Henderson, 1997, pp. 149–50; Thompson, 1984, pp. 21–2). When such topicality is combined with celebrity casting choices and rumours about personal conflicts in the leading actors' offstage lives, the draw, historically, has proven irresistible. Garrick first wrote *Catharine and Petruchio* in 1754, but it became a staple of theatre-going London only in 1756 when Kitty Clive and Henry Woodward – actors known to despise each other – took over the title roles. A slightly different dynamic has become well established in the twentieth century with famous (and famously squabbling) husband and wife teams cast as Katherine and Petruchio. One thinks, for instance, of Mary Pickford and Douglas Fairbanks; Lynn Fontanne and Alfred Lunt – a pairing that inspired Cole Porter in 1948 to write *Kiss Me Kate* (a musical dramatizing the turbulent onstage/offstage relationship of two actors starring in *The Taming of the Shrew*); Elizabeth Taylor and Richard Burton in Franco Zeffirelli's 1967 film version; and perhaps even, to add yet another metatheatrical layer, Cybill Shepherd and Bruce Willis playing Maddie Hayes and David Addison playing Katherine and Petruchio in a 1986 episode of the American television series *Moonlighting*.

The notoriety of the script, along with the publicity that surrounds celebrity actors who seem to reproduce in their own lives the fortunes of their stage characters, would certainly do nothing to hurt the play's appeal in performance. Another possible source of interest, especially for knowledgeable theatre-goers, derives from the opportunity to assess a particular production's interpretative choices in relation to a controversial storyline. *The Shrew*, with its tripartite plot structure, is an immensely flexible play – a theatrical Lego set – containing detachable pieces that can be snapped together in different ways to various effect, with the anonymous *Taming of A Shrew* functioning as a sort of bonus accessories package thrown in for free. In some cases, this creative assembly is extensive enough to be relabelled adaptation. There have been many landmark productions of this play staged and filmed around the world over the past four centuries. The five productions discussed below have been chosen for the way, considered as a group, they draw out the broad range of staging strategies and political agenda that theatre and film have brought to this difficult play. Each of them engages in a distinctive manner with the play's challenges, and each of them has proven influential, either because of its long stage run, its particular interpretative approach or, especially in the case of film and television versions, because of its continued availability to modern audiences.

Catharine and Petruchio (1754)

With the restoration of King Charles II in 1660 and the reopening of the English theatres, Shakespeare's comedy was transformed into two- and three-act farces that emphasized the comic roles either of Christopher Sly or of Grumio, Petruchio's servant. In 1754, David Garrick took *The Shrew* in a different direction, one that proved to define the play in Britain until 1844 and in the United States until 1887, after which time Garrick's treatment fell out of favour and producers began returning to Shakespeare's fuller version. Like its immediate predecessors, *Catharine and Petruchio* was offered as a short afterpiece to an evening's theatrical entertainment.

Garrick's tactic was to strip away two of Shakespeare's three plot threads, reshaping the play to focus attention exclusively on the taming of Katherina. Sly is cut, and Bianca opens the action already married to Hortensio; her other suitors, Tranio (in disguise as Lucentio), Lucentio and Gremio, disappear altogether, with the part of the music master, as a result, no longer played as a disguise role.

The action is heavily compressed over 72 hours. Petruchio woos and wins Catharine one day, and marries her the next, throwing away as burnt the meal waiting for them at his home in Verona. On the third day, Catharine is fed 'with the name of meat', fails to get a new cap and gown, accepts that the sun is the moon, and delivers a version of her speech of wifely duty when Baptista, Bianca and Hortensio turn up on a surprise visit in the play's closing moments.

This stripped down version of the story relied heavily on interpolated stage business – it is probably at this point in the play's history, for instance, that Petruchio took up his whip, a stage property that would survive in performance well into the twentieth century. One of the servants in Padua (Garrick names him Pedro) tells Grumio that his master 'shook his whip in token of his love' during the marriage ceremony (II.120–1), and the property note 'whip for Petruchio' appears alongside Petruchio's entrance to the wedding scene in a version of *Catharine and Petruchio* used by John Philip Kemble in 1788. But while ever more physical gags were introduced, Shakespeare's verbal bawdy was decorously elided, presumably to accommodate a mid-eighteenth century sense of propriety. Most notably, Petruchio's allusion to oral sex in the wooing scene becomes an offer to taste the 'honey' of Catharine's lips (I.168–70), and he promises to warm himself, not in her bed, but her arms (l. 204).

There are other ways in which Garrick, playing Petruchio to Shakespeare's Katherina, tames a froward script. In particular, he gives Catharine lines to suggest that a potentially willing bride and wife lies behind the façade of the shrew. She expresses grudging sexual attraction towards her future husband when she first sets eyes on him, admitting in an aside to the audience that 'yet the man's a man'. Her inexplicable silence in Shakespeare's text later in the same scene, when she fails to contradict Petruchio's claim that her 'no' really means 'yes', is accounted for here with her determination, again delivered as an aside, to marry and tame this suitor (l. 245). Catharine thus resolves to marry Petruchio, but will compete with him for authority, a decision implicitly encouraged by her father's threat to disinherit and turn her out of doors if she refuse to marry. The scene (and act) ends with Catharine, in soliloquy, citing revenge on both her sister and suitor as cause to marry:

> Why, yes: sister Bianca now shall see
> The poor abandoned Cath'rine, as she calls me,
> Can hold her head as high, and be as proud,
> And make her husband stoop unto her lure,
> As she, or e'er a wife in Padua.
> As double as my portion be my scorn;
> Look to your seat, Petruchio, or I throw you.
> Cath'rine shall tame this haggard; or, if she fails,
> Shall tie her tongue up and pare down her nails.
>   (ll. 278–86)

The rhyming couplet in the closing lines is telling, since it sets the stakes at double or nothing: should she lose the competition with her husband for supremacy, she plans to concede the match and surrender the weapons – her tongue and her nails – that define her as a shrew. By thus giving Catharine clear motivation first to marry, then eventually to submit to her husband's rule, Garrick tempers the politics of the taming process, with Petruchio coming to seem the husband Catharine, at some level, desired from the outset.

If Catharine seems less than fully committed to either the single or the shrewish life, Petruchio is characterized with care as a reluctant tyrant. Peter, one of his servants in Verona, elaborates on the line in Shakespeare's play that explains Petruchio's tactics – 'He kills her in her own humour' – to express surprise that 'so good and kind a master could have put on so resolute a bearing' (II.371–2). In the final act, Petruchio not only refuses Baptista's second dowry, claiming his wife is wealth enough, but ostentatiously throws off the role of the domestic bully:

> My fortune is sufficient. Her's my wealth.
> Kiss me, my Kate; and since thou art become
> So prudent, kind, and dutiful a wife,
> Petruchio here shall doff the lordly husband;
> An honest mask, which I throw off with pleasure.
> Far hence all rudeness, wilfulness, and noise,
> And be our future lives one gentle stream
> Of mutual love, compliance, and regard.
>   (ll. 266–73)

Petruchio glosses the final stage picture as one of mutuality and compromise, with Catharine, in face of such generosity, claiming to 'look with blushes on my former self' (III.275). However, the concessions, one should note, are all in one direction. As in Shakespeare's text, Petruchio 'rewards' his wife (with a kiss, a journey to the bedroom or the promise of respect) once Catharine has histrionically and publicly acknowledged herself his subject. Moreover, in Garrick's treatment, Catharine loses even the opportunity to command centre-stage. Her show-stopping 44-line monologue is not only heavily cut, but interrupted first by Petruchio and then by Bianca, a treatment that leaves the actress playing Catharine with three short speeches of six, four and nine lines, radically diminishing any potential to establish in the closing moments a powerful stage presence. On the contrary, the action firmly focuses spectators' attention on Petruchio, who is cued to '*G[o] forward with* Catharine *in his hand*' to deliver part of her speech in the manner of an epilogue:

> Such duty as the subject owes the prince,
> Even such a woman oweth to her husband.
> And when she's froward, peevish, sullen, sour,
> And not obedient to his honest will;
> What is she but a foul contending rebel
> And graceless traitor to her loving lord?
> How shameful 'tis when women are so simple
> To offer war where they should kneel for peace;
> Or seek for rule, supremacy, and sway,
> Where bound to love, to honor and obey.
>
> (ll. 277–86)

In Shakespeare's version, a spectator can wonder, along with Lucentio, if Katherina really means what she says. Here, that awkward loose end is tied up as Catharine stands silently, and obediently, by her husband's side as she listens with the rest of the audience to Petruchio enjoin female obedience by cataloguing the source of female shame.

The Taming of the Shrew (directed Sam Taylor, 1929)

Although the Pickford–Fairbanks *Shrew* made history as the first Shakespeare play to be filmed with sound, its indebtedness to the silent film tradition is evident. It was shot with minimal dialogue and an emphasis on exaggerated facial and bodily gesture in order to accommodate either a silent or sound presentation (the film was eventually released in both formats). Another legacy, that of Garrick's influential shaping of Shakespeare's play for the stage, can likewise be traced in this early black and white film. As in *Catharine and Petruchio*, Shakespeare's action is heavily cut: the subplot is condensed and simplified with Bianca courted by Hortensio, her only suitor; there is no wager scene and no extra dowry; and the Sly plot is stripped away in its entirety. There are also explicit verbal borrowings from Garrick's version, with Katherina promising in soliloquy after the wooing scene either to tame Petruchio or surrender the contest: 'Look to your seat, Petruchio, or I throw you. / Kath'rine shall tame this haggard; or, if she fails, / Shall tie her tongue up and pare down her nails.'

In keeping with long-standing stage traditions, the action is treated as broadly farcical. Petruchio cracks his now-standard whip and, as though to exaggerate the comic effect, Katherina wields her own whip with which she terrorizes her father's household. Plates are smashed against the wall and mirrors are broken; the music-master (Hortensio in disguise) is thrown down a sweeping stone staircase with the lute wrapped like a collar around his neck just as Petruchio announces that he 'woos not like a babe'; and there is elaborate business during the wedding (staged, rather than narrated, in this production) involving a discarded apple core that eventually finds its way into Gremio's trousers. This reading of the action as farce is foreshadowed by the Punch and Judy show that opens the film in which Punch gets a kiss from Judy only after he beats her with a stick. This short sketch, in effect functioning in place of Sly as the induction to the film, immediately focuses attention on the politics of the taming plot, preparing the audience for Garrick-like physical comedy.

But this early film also presents an innovative and groundbreaking departure from Garrick's afterpiece, particularly in its treatment of the actual taming process. The action set in Verona after the wedding is heavily foreshortened, with Katherina and Petruchio reaching an understanding on their first night as husband and wife. The tailor scene and exchange on the road to Padua are omitted, and the camera cuts directly from their marital bedroom to the banquet scene and Katherina's speech on wifely duty. This reconceived taming sequence is organized around two overheard soliloquies. Shortly after her arrival at Verona, Katherina, still wet, cold and filthy from her journey, is captured by the camera seated on a stool and musing silently in turn on her wedding band and whip. Just as Petruchio enters the balcony above and behind her, she repeats out loud part of the warning she issued in soliloquy after the wooing scene: 'Look to your seat, Petruchio.'

This overheard threat functions to motivate Petruchio's outlandish behaviour, setting the two of them in explicit competition for control over the other. Shrugging as though to say 'if that's the way you want it', he exits into the bedroom to re-enter a moment later cracking his whip and shouting for service. After spilling the water and throwing away their dinner as burnt, Petruchio carries his wife up to their bedroom where he ignores her in favour of a game of cards. When Katherina, in frustration, exits to get changed into a seductive negligee, Petruchio races back downstairs to finish the remains of their meal. As he pushes his plate away and delivers his soliloquy on how to 'tame a wife with kindness' to Troilus, his Great Dane, Katherina enters above on the balcony.

This film thus makes Katherina, along with the audience, privy to Petruchio's taming strategies. By denying Petruchio the rhetorical force of a soliloquy – he confides his plan to his dog, unaware of his wife's silent and knowing presence behind him – the power dynamic is reversed. Katherina's confusion and frustration immediately dissolves, and when Petruchio next enters their bedroom, she is firmly in possession of the upper hand. He slams doors and sings loudly and tunelessly while she tries to sleep, and she applauds his performance; he opens a window, letting in a cold breeze, and she opens a second one, seeming to refresh herself in face of a gale. In this context they play out a version of the sun–moon sequence. Looking out of the open window at the night sky, Petruchio says it is the sun that shines so bright, to which Katherina, slightly revising Shakespeare, replies, 'It *is* the sun, or if you please, call it a candle, I vow it shall be so for me . . . what you will have it named even that it is and so it shall be for Katherine'.

Crucially, then, Petruchio wins the power to define his wife's world within hours of their marriage, but his victory, in this reworked context, translates into a defeat. Unable to understand how she can remain poised and collected, seemingly indifferent to his bluster, Petruchio becomes increasingly perverse and violent. The moment when Katherina, holding her wounded husband against her breast, spots her whip and tosses it on the open fire is the turning-point of the film, and it precisely defines the terms of their future relationship. Her strategy is to get her way by only seeming to give her husband his. 'The *sun* is shining bright?', he asks her anxiously, and she soothes him with the assurance, 'Ay, the blessèd sun.' The audience infers that this swashbuckling bully is merely humoured by his loving, and more intelligent, wife. This interpretation is consistent with production choices elsewhere in the film that serve to belittle the wife-tamer. The camera catches Gremio and Hortensio exchanging looks throughout Petruchio's whip-cracking 'Have I not heard lions roar' monologue, and in a later scene Gremio bursts out laughing when Petruchio says 'How I long to have some gr-r-r-apple with her!', pointedly mocking his friend's elaborately rolled 'r' with the interpolated line 'For all the world I would not have some gr-r-r-apple with her!' Even at her wedding, the frustrated Katherina makes Petruchio the butt of the joke by impersonating his swaggering stance and booming laugh.

Petruchio, a two-dimensional farcical caricature of the ambitious adventurer, is impervious to Katherina's hostility: she slaps him not once but four times during the wooing scene, and he simply laughs at her (the threat that he will 'cuff' her if she strike again is cut). She whips him while he tells her father how well they have agreed and again he remains oblivious to her violence. He will not be moved, as he predicts, by Katherina's fury, and she is given away, kicking and biting, by a relieved father. Unable to cross such a husband, Katherina can achieve mastery only by stepping around him. This is the interpretative context that gives meaning in the final scene to the famous 'Pickford wink'. At her enjoinder to women to 'serve, love, and obey', she pauses to wink at the incredulous Bianca, who is immediately transformed into a knowing participant in her sister's game. The moment is captured by the camera as a shot/reverse shot sequence, thus creating the impression that Katherina secretly confides in Bianca (and so the audience) the true secret of a happy marriage.

Shakespeare's play is worked through to a very different interpretation of marital harmony than the image of civic and domestic order provided by Garrick. Like Garrick though, and despite the ironic delivery of Katherina's final speech, the Pickford–Fairbanks production ultimately grounds marital success in romantic love. At the end of their first meeting, Pickford is swept into Fairbanks's arms in a long kiss. Katherina pounds his arm a few times with her fist, and then, reminiscent of the moment in *Catharine and Petruchio* when Catherine admiringly notes 'yet the man's a man', her arm slowly relaxes. As she steps away from the embrace, she regards Petruchio with stunned surprise before recovering her composure. The motherly embrace in which Katherina enfolds Petruchio on their wedding night and her broad wink to Bianca during the banquet scene are thus accompaniments to, rather than substitutes for, erotic desire. Where Garrick presents a vision of mutuality founded on reason, Taylor finds loving compromise facilitated by deception. The Punch and Judy show with which the film begins captures the troubling belief that women only respect men who enforce obedience and sexual intimacy, but its broad farce elides entirely a rather more complex interpretation of the shifting power dynamics between husband and wife.

Charles Marowitz, *The Shrew* (1974) and the BBC–Time/Life, *Taming of the Shrew* (dir. Jonathan Miller, 1980)

The physical comedy which was the key to successful productions of Shakespeare's *Shrew* through to the early twentieth century was resisted by key productions in the last half of the twentieth century.

Charles Marowitz and Jonathan Miller, to take two distinct but related examples, turned away from farce and irony to explore what happens if one accepts at face value Petruchio's assertion that Katherina is a belonging over which he is entitled to command with an 'awful rule'. If the action in these productions was humorous, it was only incidentally so, as Marowitz and Miller drew out a seriousness of tone more in keeping with wife-beating ballads of the mid-sixteenth century or accounts of domestic abuse in their own time than the conventions of romantic comedy. In place of comedy, these directors offered a sustained exploration of the historical and psychological implications of an imagined world in which a husband is given the power to assert absolute authority over his wife.

Marowitz's *Shrew* (he gave his production of Shakespeare's play an abbreviated title) was first performed in England in 1974 before touring throughout Europe, Australia and North America, and it is one of a series of collage treatments of Shakespeare's drama produced by this director/playwright throughout the 1960s and 1970s. The way Marowitz elides the induction scenes and cuts away all suitors to Bianca apart from Hortensio is in keeping with traditions of production that date back to the eighteenth century, showing striking similarities to the work of Garrick and Taylor. But other modifications to the script radically undermine these directors' visions of domestic reciprocity and marital accommodation. An important thread in late twentieth-century criticism emphasizes the play's brutality (see Chapter 6, pp. 152–3). A perception of the violence that underpins Shakespeare's play has inspired various stage interpretations, with the Marowitz *Shrew* gaining notoriety as one of the earliest, and most influential, of these productions.

Petruchio, motivated entirely by Katherina's immense fortune, is characterized by a menacing, thug-like behaviour that intimidates both his future wife and her father. Marowitz inserts stage directions throughout the printed text that document how he directed key moments in performance. Baptista's claim, for instance, that 'Katherine . . . is not for [Petruchio's] turn' is met with a 'threatening silence' and 'grim, dead-eyed' stare (p. 137). The unsettled father is then seated by Grumio and Hortensio on a stool beside Petruchio, with the actors seeming to gang up on Baptista by gathering around him 'rather too closely' (p. 138). The wooing scene that follows is less flirtatious than dangerous as Petruchio, '[f]inding it difficult to play the game' (p. 142), ends the banter by grabbing Katherina's crotch, a 'brutish move' that leaves her 'momentarily stunned' (p. 143).

The role-play device which is cut from the subplot is trans-ferred to the so-called 'taming school' in Verona where Grumio and Hortensio, assuming different masks, play the parts of the tailor, cap-maker, cook and servants. There is, in effect, no house-hold for Katherina to join after marriage, but only a staged enact-ment of a household, with Petruchio's friends conspiring to break his recalcitrant wife. After being denied both clothing and food upon her arrival, Katherina *'peers into their faces; i.e.* HORTENSIO's *and* GRUMIO's *masks'* (p. 164), unsuccessfully trying to see past their disguises. As she exits to bed, the three men slowly turn to smile at one another.

The journey back to Padua is likewise handled entirely through role-play, with Petruchio and Hortensio 'trot[ting] in place as if on horseback' (p. 173), forcing a confused and increasingly vulnerable Katherina to play along. She finally collapses after her encounter with Grumio, now in disguise as Petruchio's father, Antonio: *'Slowly,* KATE *draws herself up. A high-pitched crescendo whistle is heard inside her head which the audience also hears. It builds to an impossible pitch and then something snaps. All lights go red'* (p. 176). As though in a fairy-tale or dream, Katherina is suddenly surrounded by her father, Grumio and Hortensio, who, borrowing dialogue from Shakespeare's second Induction, tend on her every desire, offering her food, drink, music and clothing. This rearranged text thus explicitly links the false world of Verona with the false world created by the lord for Christopher Sly. Katherina, like Sly, gratefully accepts the pleasing deception as truth: 'I do not sleep. I see, I hear, I speak. / I smell sweet savors and I feel soft things' (p. 177). This benevolence is shattered moments later when Petruchio, entering the enactment and taking from his wife the part of Sly, asks her to 'come now to bed'. Katherina's attempt to avoid sexual intercourse by speaking the excuses of Shakespeare's page, Bartholomew, prompts a scene of brutal onstage violence in which she is held down and raped by Petruchio:

(KATE *is backed over to the table and then thrown down over it. Her servants and* BAPTISTA *hold her wrists to keep her secure.* PETRUCHIO *looms up behind her and whips up her skirts ready to do buggery. As he inserts, an ear-piercing, electronic whistle rises to a crescendo pitch.* KATE's *mouth is wild and open, and it appears as if the impossible sound is issuing from her lungs.*)
Blackout. (p. 178)

The next and final scene, staged as a tribunal, shows Katherina, broken and wearing 'a simple, shapeless institutional-like garment' (p. 178), mechanically reciting a speech of obedience she has learned by rote. *The Shrew* drains Shakespeare's drama of any potential for light-hearted comic romance. Petruchio's taming strategies are presented not only as sadistic and self-serving, but as a form of psychological torture that culminates in a manipulative, destructive theatricality associated with twentieth-century show trials. Marowitz's commentary on the gender politics of Shakespeare's play is set alongside an interpolated subplot, original to his staging, that satirizes modern marriage as 'the inescapable 20th century compromise' (p. 20). Three scenes dramatizing the modern-day courtship of a wealthy 'Girl' and commoner 'Boy' – characters played by the same actors who play Bianca and Hortensio – are interspersed among the scenes of Katherina's taming. Despite an emotionally and sometimes physically abusive relationship, the generic 'Girl' and 'Boy' eventually marry. These parallel plots are brought together in the play's closing moments with the modern couple, dressed in their wedding apparel, smiling out to an imaginary camera just as Katherina completes her speech of obedience.

The effect of these juxtaposed plots is more complex than any simple conflation of historically remote situations. The point is not to assert that over four hundred years things have remained 'just the same', but to investigate rhetoric about romantic love and the institution of marriage in two related, yet distinct, contexts. Whereas the Girl and Boy tell an everyday story of compromise and mediocrity, Katherina is exceptional; all come to seem brutalized in different ways by marriage. By refusing those stage choices that might allow an audience to believe that Katherina either falls in love with her husband or benefits from her experiences at the taming school, Marowitz creates a nightmarish world that sets into relief the way romantic love and marriage (fail to) function in his own time as solutions to exploitative situations of class and gender inequality.

Jonathan Miller, by contrast, puts historical context to very different use by attempting to approach the play through late Elizabethan, rather than late-twentieth century, assumptions about marriage and the family. He directed *The Taming of the Shrew* three times, twice for the British stage (1972, 1987) and once for television (1980). Miller's interpretation of the play for television, preserved on video-cassette as part of the BBC–Time/Life dramatization of Shakespeare's canon, is widely available in schools and libraries and thus remains a massively influential staging. Unlike productions that drastically simplify the Bianca disguise plot, Miller – no doubt guided by the series' full-text mandate – stages the story of Baptista and his two daughters in its entirety. Curiously, though, not even the institutional pressure to televise full-text productions could prevent the exclusion of the two Induction scenes. Miller's argument was that the Christopher Sly material, a self-conscious stage device 'that brings the audience into close identification with some person who is like them', is incompatible with the medium: 'It would be on television a little extra programme tagged on before the programme proper actually begins' (Miller, 1988, p. 201). He likewise cut the Induction scenes from both of his stage productions, a consistency of interpretative approach that perhaps implies that Shakespeare's preliminary matter sits uneasily with Miller's larger conception of the play (Schafer, 2002, p. 73).

The idea behind all three of Miller's productions was to try to recover in performance the way Shakespeare might have thought about the family. Miller was explicitly hostile to feminist stagings, arguing that productions that 'hijack the work to make it address current problems about women's place in society, become boring, thin and tractarian' (Miller, 1988, p. 200). For Miller, the play 'is about the setting up of a sober household and the necessity for marital obedience in order to maintain it' (Miller, 1981, p. 138):

> [Shakespeare] underwrote the idea that the state, whether it was the small state of the family or the larger state of the country, required and needed the unquestioned authority of some sort of sovereign to whom everyone

could defer. . . . Now, that's not something which we acknowledge or accept, but . . . [i]f we wish to make all plays from the past conform to our ideals and what we think the state or the family ought to be like, then we're simply rewriting all plays and turning them into modern ones. (Miller, 1981, p. 140)

This discussion of history and politics, indebted to such texts as 'A Homily against Disobedience and Wilful Rebellion' (see Chapter 3, pp. 110–12), is reminiscent of C. S. Lewis's view that modern readers may find *The Taming of the Shrew* 'startling', but that 'those who cannot face such startling should not read old books' (see Chapter 6, p. 155). Miller's production seeks to present to a modern audience a foreign historical moment, interpreting the taming of Katherina as a benefit to society on the grounds that actual Elizabethans would have advocated, with Petruchio, a husband's 'right supremacy' within marriage. The self-reflexive nature of the Sly frame – the way it comments on the inset action, insisting that it is just a fiction – undermines an approach that constructs theatre as 'a form of ethnology' (Miller, 1988, p. 201), a means by which spectators can learn about the past. It is perhaps not surprising then that the production locates the audience from the outset within the fiction of the Padua world.

Ironically, the realization that Miller's conception of an Elizabethan world-view only works if the Induction scenes are cut suggests strongly that his production is no less an imposition on a 400-year old text than the feminist interpretations he dismisses as 'silly' on grounds of anachronism. The performance of 'history' is always a staged effect, limited by existing means of theatrical production, inspired by recourse to current scholarship on the past, and moulded on the assumptions and politics of one's own historical moment. As Elizabeth Schafer aptly comments, 'How precisely Miller expected to transcend his own cultural specificity, accessing *The Shrew* with no interference whatsoever from "what we think now" is not explained' (p. 73). The actors wear period costumes and the Padua sets, in particular, are influenced by Dutch Renaissance paintings. This imprecise muddle of national and cultural influence – English playwright, Italian setting, Dutch pictorial allusions, all located within an ill-concealed studio set – reproduces history as nothing more precise than a generic 'Renaissance' effect. Moreover, the twentieth century keeps intruding into the sixteenth-century fiction: Biondello chews gum and walks with a laddish swagger, and Tranio's working-class status remains audible in the glottal stops that dog his laboured attempt at an upper-class English accent. These sorts of socio-economic details mark the production, inevitably, as a careful negotiation of the signs of identity in the reign not of Queen Elizabeth I but of Queen Elizabeth II.

Tone is likewise shaped by this conception of the play as a moral narrative about social order. Petruchio's soliloquies are self-reflective and internalized; Katherina, sitting motionless in a chair and her face in close-up, asks in a defeated voice if Petruchio married her to famish her; and even Hortensio, disguised as the music master, whispers in Baptista's ear rather than shouts the abuse he suffered at Katherina's hands. The film's few moments of broad physical comedy are largely restricted to the disguise plot. A camped-up Hortensio semaphores his true identity to Bianca while mouthing his gamut, and sprays Tranio with spit as he indignantly promises to abandon his suit of marriage; he is also the only character to break the film's fictional space by addressing the camera. Such business, however, remains incidental. Even the false Vincentio device becomes the stuff of conflict rather than laughter. Lucentio, evidently not told in advance about the scam, is kept in view in the background throughout the Pedant's encounter with Baptista at Act IV, scene iv, visibly angered both by Tranio's presumption and the stranger's imposture.

The 'tremendously flamboyant, twinkle-eyed cavalier image of Petruchio' (Miller, 1981, pp. 138–9) is abandoned altogether, along with the rough-house that frequently accompanies the taming plot. Petruchio – played by the British comedy actor John Cleese – is characterized by a quiet stillness that can seem icy, and even menacing. He grasps Tranio firmly by the arm in I.ii as he explains how Baptista keeps his younger daughter from all suitors until his elder daughter is married; when he eventually releases his grip, Tranio massages his arm while offering to subsidize Petruchio's courtship. His strength, and Tranio's evident pain, creates a perception of unwelcome force in the next scene when Petruchio similarly takes Katherina in hand to tell her how 'affable' he finds her manner. This hint of violence is not limited to moments of physical contact. When he first arrives in Padua, Petruchio uses sustained eye contact and a measured stride to intimidate and silence an impertinent Grumio. As Tranio and Gremio rush to the seated Petruchio in the wooing scene, repeating Katherina's promise to see him hanged on Sunday, his tone suddenly shifts from jovial ease to threatening danger as he quietly demands of them, 'If she and I be pleased, what's that to you?' In the long pause that follows, Tranio and Gremio stiffen and pull back slightly, caught in Petruchio's cold stare.

Petruchio's interest in Katherina is motivated entirely by money. Katherina's reasons for marriage are less obvious; she seems to detest Petruchio, yet she stands silently in his arms, staring into the middle distance, while her father agrees to the match. This is a difficult moment for any production, as it seems inconceivable that Katherina would fail to contradict his false account of their private conversation. Sarah Badel plays Katherina as an emotionally damaged figure who, almost despite herself, can only handle her anger by harming herself and those around her. After beating Bianca as she demands to know which of her suitors she loves best, Katherina pulls away to face the camera, holding her head in her hands as though in fear of slipping entirely out of control; as her father reproaches her, she falls into a disturbing rage, weeping and screaming as she exits the room. An important trigger for Katherina's violence in this production is Baptista's preference for his younger daughter. Baptista and Bianca are shown interacting lovingly with each other in the opening scene, with Katherina, hovering in the background, pointedly excluded. The effect of such favouritism is captured moments later as Katherina stands in the foreground, eating an apple, anxiously listening to her father behind her tell his neighbours how he plans to secure tutors for his younger daughter. Baptista's dismissive instruction to Katherina, telling her to remain outdoors while he joins Bianca in the house, thus provides merely the immediate catalyst to a jealous rage that has been building throughout the scene.

This troubling family dynamic provides the subtext to Katherina's otherwise unexpected lack of resistance in the wooing and wedding scenes. Katherina, the unloved daughter, is portrayed as emotionally broken before, not after, she meets Petruchio. In such circumstances the so-called 'taming school' becomes a form of extended therapy, characterized, strangely, by Petruchio-as-therapist occasionally making clucking chicken noises at his wife, a mocking in-joke he happens on during their first encounter. As Miller explains in an interview, Petruchio 'holds a mirror up to her. It's a technique child therapists sometimes use today, and this is where Shakespeare is so shrewd. Far from the taming of a shrew, then, this play is, in fact, about the teaching of a shrew, or the treatment of a shrew by allowing her to see her own image through someone who, quite clearly, adores her from the beginning' (Miller, 1981, p. 140).

There is something chilling, however, almost Marowitz-like, about Katherina's enforced behaviour modification, particularly in the way the film's set and costume design seems to play on a mistrust of institutions and a fear of the abuse of institutional authority. The Padua sets are characterized by warm colours and open spaces; the interior of Baptista's home, elegantly furnished and deliberately reminiscent of a Vermeer painting, consists of 'ordinary rectangular rooms where the space is quite readily "readable." There is a readily intelligible perspective, a vanishing point which is quite clearly visible, and all is clearly lit' (Miller, 1981, p. 138). Petruchio's home, by contrast, is an attic filled with dark corners. The spectator's first encounter with Katherina's new home is by means of a camera set near the floor behind the fireplace, a sort of rat's-eye view on a bare, cold and forbidding room; the wind blows, and in the distance one hears dogs barking. The inability to see clearly the size or shape of the rooms, and the tendency to film the scenes in Verona as foreground surrounded by a black, impenetrable background, places spectators in the same confused position as Katherina, unable to find their bearings in unfamiliar surroundings. This sense of powerlessness is further emphasized at the beginning of Act IV, scene iii (the tailor scene) when Katherina is discovered seated in a chair dressed in a shapeless beige shift that keeps slipping off the shoulder. Surrounded by fully clothed men, her costume, something between a nightie and a hospital gown, marks her as the patient who never leaves – or perhaps is not allowed to leave – the house.

However, by the time she returns to her family Katherina is

composed and relaxed, evidently at peace both with herself and her husband after a sudden breakthrough on the road to Padua. Her reformation from shrew to loving wife is confirmed with kisses in the street and at the banquet that are so prolonged that bystanders, in order not to seem voyeurs, have to look away and occupy themselves with other activities. This performance choice does little to dispel one's unease about Petruchio's Svengali-like control over his wife. Bianca's transformation is no less remarkable. She is praised at the beginning of the film as the ideal of female virtue, but a steamy Latin lesson in which her tutor's hand steals towards her breast suggests early on that she is sexually available. Her jibe at Gremio during the banquet is staged as the only inappropriately sharp quip, and Petruchio, quick to spot a shrew, rebukes her. These hints of disorder finally culminate in flat disobedience to her husband. The example of Bianca thus constructs female sexuality and voice as always potentially unruly – shrews, one infers, might be anywhere.

The conservatism of this reading is pointed by Katherina's delivery of the final speech. It is shot almost entirely at medium range, with the camera pulling out only once – to frame Bianca and Lucentio in the foreground – when Katherina likens a wife's obedience to her husband to the duty the subject owes the prince. She remains seated at the end of the banquet table, a significant production choice as it means that Petruchio, positioned next to her, can be kept always in the shot. The speech plays, in effect, as a duet, and spectators, reading the frame from left to right (from Petruchio to Katherina), hear her words as authorized by her intently listening husband. An added piece of business in the film's closing moments – the wedding party joining together to sing a Puritan hymn based on a psalm praising the family – imposes comic harmony on the action.

In different ways and to very different purposes, *The Shrew* and the BBC–Time/Life television production stage Shakespeare's play as a sombre, even punitive, investigation of gender relations. Whereas Marowitz presents Petruchio's behaviour as psychopathic and Katherina's fate as tragic, Miller, trying to direct his way back into Shakespeare's England, validates Katherina's 'cure' as personally redemptive and socially beneficial.

The Taming of the Shrew (dir. Richard Monette, 1988)

Christopher Sly made his post-Restoration reappearance on the stage in 1844 in Benjamin Webster's production of *The Taming of the Shrew* at the Haymarket Theatre, but it was not until the next century, in a production directed by Martin Harvey at the Prince of Wales Theatre in 1913, that he sat in view of the audience to watch the show in its entirety, thus firmly establishing the Italian action as a play-within-a-play. It was at this time, presumably in an effort to find something for Sly to do, that the practice of raiding *The Taming of a Shrew* for dialogue to supplement Shakespeare's truncated framing device began. Keeping Sly on stage offers productions the opportunity to reflect on theatre as art, a self-conscious metatheatrical effect put to good use, for example, by John Barton in his Royal Shakespeare Company (RSC) production of 1960. This layering effect can also act as a buffer from the politics of the inset play. 'The Taming of the Shrew' becomes 'just' an entertainment designed to appeal to a tinker who, failing to recognize the difference between life and art, foolishly believes he now knows how to tame a wife – the theatre audience supposedly knows better.

The Sly frame has assumed over the years many shapes, from the thatched Elizabethan inn of Barton's 1960 production, to Bill Alexander's updating of the lord and his entourage at the RSC in 1992 as 'Hooray Henrys' – upper-class English snobs – who encounter Sly passed out in the street and decide to take him home to 'play with his mind' (the dialogue in the Induction scenes was modernized). Another popular treatment of the Induction, one anticipated by Jayne Sears in an essay published in 1966, is to present the Italian action as Sly's dream. Sears's argument is that the Induction scenes might point to a piece of now lost stage business in which Sly falls asleep on stage, having watched only the scene in which Baptista removes Bianca from society until a husband is found for Katharina. What follows is not the actors' play, but Sly's dream, starring Sly himself as Petruchio.

There is no evidence that the comedy was ever played this way on the Elizabethan stage, but the suggestion provides rich fodder for modern production. The inset action becomes Sly's fantasy, the enacted wish fulfilment of a disempowered man. Michael Bogdanov famously used the device in his 1978 RSC production, further unsettling the distinction between art and life by beginning the first Induction, in modernized English, among the theatre audience. Jonathan Pryce, costumed as a drunken, belligerent theatre-goer, verbally attacked a female usher (played by Paola Dionisotti, who would eventually take the part of Katherina), before stumbling onto the stage and tearing down the set. This Sly/Petruchio viciously exploited his new-found power to abuse both wife and servants, an interpretation that prompted Michael Billington in the review quoted at the beginning of this chapter to query why we should continue to perform this play at all.

Where Bogdanov emphasized the play's potential cruelty, Richard Monette used the dream device to very different effect. Monette's production, staged in 1988 at the Stratford Festival of Canada and televized the following year by the Canadian Broadcasting Corporation, offers a key point of comparison with the other productions discussed in this chapter. Its blend of comedy and sentimentality shaped a staging seductive enough to persuade a late-twentieth century audience to accept, without resort to irony, the politics of a headstrong wife tamed by her husband. The treatment of the Induction as Sly's dream was made explicit through the omission of the lord and his entourage. Sly (Colm Feore), dressed in modern casual clothing and swearing loudly in Italian, was thrown onto a bare stage by two bartenders accompanied by the hostess. Modifying a line from Shakespeare and staggering under the influence of drink, Sly propositions the attractive, but unreceptive, Hostess, asking her to 'come to my cold bed and warm thee'. What follows is a monologue composed of a pastiche of lines from the second Induction; spoken to empty space, Sly's objections to sack and claim to have no more shoes than feet and sometimes more feet than shoes seem the incoherent ramblings of a drunk. As he passes out on the darkened stage, eerie music and a harlequin picked out in a spotlight signal the transition into a dream world – when the lights come up again, a neon sign above a vibrant street scene announces the location as 'PADUA'.

Sly, the late-night drunk unable to pick up a woman he finds sexually attractive, is transformed into Petruchio, the 'great Hercules' able to woo, wed and finally tame Baptista's domineering daughter – a part played by Goldie Semple who, doubling the Hostess, previously rejected Sly's advances. Sly thus disappears entirely into the inset narrative, only to re-emerge briefly in the closing moments in the form of a silent epilogue. As the wedding party exits in song, the stage returns to the half-light of the Induction scene, and Sly, once again in the clothes in which he was thrown out of the bar, stands looking out at the spectators in quiet confusion, eventually staggering downstage to exit the play as though through the world of the theatre audience.

In Monette's hands, Sly's dream space set out to inspire in the theatre audience, no less than Katherina, a playful and creative engagement with games. Set in Italy in the 1950s, this was a pacey, stylish production filled with visual gags aimed at a 1980s audience. Lucentio and Tranio drive into Padua in a little red car displaying 'PISA' licence plates; Petruchio roars in on a Vespa; Tranio as Lucentio flashes his American Express card as he offers to buy his fellow suitors a round of drinks; and Biondello uses a telephone to tell Lucentio (who picks up from Bianca's bedroom) to elope with his mistress. Such details seem to wink knowingly at the theatre audience, inviting them to share in the fun. Passages of Italian dialogue scattered throughout the production, sometimes extended and frequently laced with obscenity, both contribute to this effect of self-aware theatricality and establish a cultural framework in which hot-tempered words and loud arguments are nothing out of the ordinary.

Katherina enters her first scene dressed in red, a stereotypical costuming choice that the wit of her subsequent actions belies. The way she casually grinds out her cigarette on the fender of Lucentio's sports car, or tortures Bianca by dismembering her teddy bear, arm by arm, leg by leg, suggests a character both exceptional and, in her way, charismatic. It is this originality to which Petruchio seems to respond, even before they meet, as he bites his lip, hardly able to contain his laughter, when Hortensio in disguise as the music tutor tells how he 'stood amazèd for a while, / As on a pillory, looking through the lute' after Katherina smashed her instrument over his head. As he turns to find Katherina standing behind him later in the scene, this Petruchio, momentarily lost for words, falls in love at first sight, an effect pointed thereafter with long pauses before 'the prettiest Kate in Christendom' and 'Yet [thy beauty sounded] not so deeply as to thee belongs'.

Petruchio's characterization is in many ways the key to this production's effect of gentle romance. He seemed keen from the outset to marry Katherina, but by downplaying his fortune-hunting motives and delivering the 'fear boys with bugs' speech with an understated simplicity, he seemed neither a bully nor a swaggerer. Mention of his father's death, instead of being played for laughs as in the Miller and Marowitz productions, seemed painful both to Petruchio and those who knew his father, and when the newlyweds arrive at Verona, Katherina encounters 'cousin Ferdinand', a disabled relative for whom Petruchio provides. Performance decisions such as these create a perception of the wife-tamer as a man with the emotional capacity to care deeply about loved ones. Taming, in this context, comes to seem a matter of persuading Katherina to let down her guard enough to allow her to fall in love with her husband. The sense that this is, above all, a shared trial is emphasized by the revision of 'she' to 'we' in the 'politic reign' soliloquy: 'We eat no meat today, nor none shall eat. / Last night we slept not, nor tonight we shall not' (IV.i.183–4).

The turning-point in their relationship occurs in the sun–moon scene, but Katherina's concession to her husband's will is carefully prepared for during the tailor scene. Petruchio continues to seem an unwilling tamer (a fleeting look of pain, for instance, crosses his face as his wife complains of her hunger), while Katherina, beating her husband with her fists after the tailor's exit, momentarily relaxes into his embrace before pulling away from him again. The moment she chooses to agree that the sun is the moon is played with humour and affection, and the entrance of the cigar-smoking Vincentio allows Katherina, in a ludicrous description of him as 'fresh and sweet', to mock gently her husband's perverse will. Semple's Katherina, bringing to life critical perspectives that find in this play a loving mutuality that grows out of shared games, is liberated by her husband's taming strategies into a rewarding and productive relationship with her family and acquaintances.

The final speech is thus played as a love letter to her husband. And yet, as in the sun–moon scene, this Katherina, though obedient, seems constantly to assess rather than blindly accommodate her husband's will. She heavily emphasizes, for example, a wife's necessary obedience to her husband's 'honest' will while looking over at a Petruchio suddenly ashamed to have insisted on 'more sign of her obedience'. The tone, however, is kept light and forgiving, as though to underscore a spirit of give-and-take. When she speaks of a husband as one that 'cares for thee, / And for thy maintenance', she crosses to stand behind her father, and rests her hands on his shoulders. This gesture implicitly, and in a very personal way, acknowledges the hard work and sacrifice on behalf of their families made by an earlier generation of husbands. Petruchio and Baptista are moved to tears by Katherina's speech, while Grumio on the margins of the scene histrionically blows his nose. As the wedding guests follow Petruchio and Katherina off the stage, a little girl, caught in a spot, breaks off to pick up her doll, a moment that summons up not only the possibility of reproduction within marriage, but extends the moral of Katherina's words to future generations of girls who will grow up to become wives.

Monette's *Shrew* presented a deeply conservative interpretation of gender relations, sugar-coating female submission to husbands and fathers with playfulness, sentimentality and comic convention. The interpretation is powerful, or perhaps invidious is the better word, because it makes wife-taming feel so good. The troubling ideological assumptions that have made this play come to seem problematic are still firmly in place, as Katherina remains her husband's ox, his ass, his any thing, married against her will. But the production seeks to persuade spectators to overlook these details as irrelevant since, happily, Petruchio's will seems, ultimately, to coincide exactly with that of his wife.

Some Conclusions

This discussion of five productions staged or filmed since the middle of the eighteenth century illustrates how difficult it is to talk of a performance residing in, or inherent in, the text. Shakespeare's text, while guiding performance, inevitably prompts from modern theatre practitioners creative input that exceeds anything one can discern in the words on the page. What will Petruchio wear to his wedding? Are Bianca and the Widow convinced by Katherina's speech – and how might this response be conveyed to an audience without benefit of words? Inspiration is not entirely dependent on the text. Original business that works at a remove from the dialogue – an added song, a striking gesture or use of a prop, extended silent interaction between two or more characters – can frequently prompt a reassessment of text, character and/or situation. Even the question of which words on the page will be delivered in performance is a matter of interpretation. Each of these five productions – including the one committed, ostensibly, to a full-text staging – shaped the spoken dialogue with care to communicate to the audience a specific reading of the action. Such intervention might be as subtle as changing individual words (revising 'she' to 'we' in Petruchio's 'politic reign' soliloquy in Act IV), or as drastic as reconceiving entirely the disguise subplot.

The Taming of the Shrew emerges from these treatments as a farce, a romantic comedy, a moralizing exploration of sixteenth-century attitudes to marriage and authority, and even a tragedy. Studying a play's production history suggests things to do, not just with texts, but with the tools of performance such as voice, gesture, set and costuming. Reading for performance transfers the creative activity to readers who, unlike theatre practitioners who are required at some point to settle on particular choices, have the freedom to consider, and reconsider, multiple theatrical options and their interpretative implications.

5 The Play on Screen

Two films in addition to the Taylor and Miller productions (see Chapter 4, 'Key Productions and Performances') are still readily available to viewers. Franco Zeffirelli's 1967 production, starring Elizabeth Taylor and Richard Burton, sets the action in Renaissance Italy. Sly is cut, and the disguise plot surrounding Bianca is heavily condensed as part of a larger strategy of shifting the focus more firmly to the taming plot – Bianca's music and Latin lessons are only glimpsed in passing, while the wedding of Katherina and Petruchio is staged in its entirety. The marriage is agreed after Katherina is locked in a room by Petruchio (this is the reason why she is unable to contradict his claim that she desires to marry him), and she watches him through a stained-glass window as he negotiates the agreement with her father. After he exits, a long silence followed by a faint smile playing across her face suggests that she is not an entirely unwilling bride. A flurry of housekeeping the day after her arrival in Verona, and a shot at the wedding banquet that captures her gazing fondly on small children playing with dogs, reinforce the idea that this particular shrew secretly longs for her own home and family.

Such moments prepare the ground for a final speech that is delivered with simple sincerity. Petruchio, having proposed the wager out of stung pride, seems uneasy about whether his wife will indeed be commanded. Once she arrives, dragging with her the other two wives, Katherina reprimands the women without any prompting from her husband. These performance choices, perhaps paradoxically, create for Katherina a stronger sense of agency: she continues to make her own decisions. The film's final moments complement this interpretation as Petruchio is forced – as he was forced during the wooing scene – to chase after his wife, this time through a sea of laughing women standing between him and the bedroom door.

10 *Things I Hate about You*, directed by Gil Junger (1999), wittily reworks Shakespeare's play as a high school comedy romance. Cameron (Lucentio) is the sweet, slightly goofy new kid who is introduced to 'Padua High' by a nerd called Michael (Tranio) who aspires to a prestigious business school. Gremio is translated into the rich, good-looking, sexually ruthless high school senior, Joey, on whom Bianca, a pretty junior, has a crush. When Bianca's father (a single parent) changes the house rule from 'no dating' to 'Bianca can date when Kat does', Joey bribes Verona (the Petruchio character, played by Heath Ledger) to ask Kat out on a date, and eventually to the prom. Kat (Julia Stiles), an articulate feminist with a hot temper who reads Sylvia Plath, listens to girl-bands and plans to attend Sarah Lawrence (a progressive East coast university) after graduating from high school, seems to have little interest in dating anyone.

Part of the pleasure of this film for Shakespeare scholars comes from marking where it diverges from *The Shrew*, and tracing how Junger finds modern analogues for Shakespeare's characters and relationships within an American high school context. Kat and Verona's first date – at a paintball complex – reproduces the Act IV hostilities between the characters, physically situating their scenes of conflict and competition within a context of play and shared games. The chase is temporarily suspended when they collapse into bales of hay, one of the course's obstacles. Their first kiss is thus situated within a knowing filmic allusion to the famous moment in the Taylor–Burton film when the lovers – Petruchio in hot pursuit of Katherina – fall through the roof of a barn.

The politics of the taming plot are made more palatable to a modern audience. Kat chooses of her own will to date (she feels sorry for a younger sister otherwise grounded throughout her adolescence), and clear motivation is found for her angry behaviour (her secret is that she lost her virginity years ago to Joey, the Gremio character, who only dated her for sex). As with the Garrick, Pickford–Fairbanks and Taylor–Burton productions, then, this Katherina at some level comes to seem, despite her protests in favour of the single life, ready to encounter her Petruchio. Verona likewise comes to belie his tough exterior and intimidating reputation: he gives up smoking, reveals he spent the previous year not in prison but caring for an ill grandfather, and in the closing scene makes amends for the bribe (which Kat finds out about at the prom) by buying her an expensive guitar, and so encouraging her to start her own band.

Even Bianca, presented at the outset as spoiled and self-centred, is brought within, rather than excluded from, the comic resolution. As in *The Shrew*, she acts as a foil to Katherina, eventually taking over elements of her sister's defiance and hostility. Her aggression, however, is directed exclusively at the manipulative and violent Joey (she twice punches him in the face at the ball, before kneeing him in the groin), and in defence of her new boyfriend, Cameron. Spectators are thus positioned to applaud, rather than deplore, her new-found spirit. Significantly, her father endorses her actions, praising her for becoming more like her 'shrewish' elder sister.

10 *Things I Hate about You* is a smart and innovative treatment of Shakespeare's play that foregrounds the gender and class preoccupations of *The Shrew* by translating them into a modern context. Perhaps even more importantly, by reworking the taming plot within the conventions of Hollywood romance – boy meets girl, boy falls in love with girl, boy gets girl – the film, in its very capacity to provide pleasure, makes visible the ideological constraints of critical assertions of romantic love. In this regard, it stands as an important interpretative counterpoint to stagings as politically diverse as those of Marowitz and Monette (see Chapter 4).

6 Critical Assessment

'Who is the shrew, and why does she need taming?' These questions, prompted by Shakespeare's title, go to the heart of the critical debate surrounding *The Taming of the Shrew*. The most obvious character to be identified with the eponymous 'shrew' is Katherina, Baptista's elder, supposedly unmarriageable daughter, whose behaviour is described by those around her as 'curst and shrewd'. Shrews begin to proliferate, however, by the closing scene, with the qualities that initially earned Katherina this label – she opens the play unruly, disobedient and argumentative – now transferred to other female characters. One shrew is evidently tamed, only to have two more (Bianca and the Widow) spring up in her place.

An even more enduring difficulty lies in the second question, in finding a justification of the process by which the socially disruptive woman is tamed. Germaine Greer, one of the play's more unlikely apologists, celebrates Shakespeare's 'theory of marriage' in her landmark feminist treastise *The Female Eunuch* (1980), describing Katherina as having 'uncommon good fortune': 'Kate's speech at the close of the play is the greatest defense of Christian monogamy ever written. It rests upon the role of a husband as protector and friend, and it is valid because Kate has a man who is capable of being both, for Petruchio is both gentle and strong' (p. 206). Perhaps one can assume Katherina is tamed for her own good – that she is happier as a result of it, or even secretly desires marriage to Petruchio; or perhaps she only pretends to submit to her husband's rule, and isn't tamed at all. Perhaps she has to be tamed in Shakespeare's story because an early modern hierarchical order demands that women should be obedient to their husbands; or perhaps the answer, more pragmatically, is simply that

Shakespeare's plot conforms to the traditional narrative trajectory of well-known folktale material.

Shakespeare's story about a husband who subordinates to his will a wife who refuses to defer to male authority taps into what still remains today an unresolved debate about ideal gender relations between the sexes, especially within marriage. *The Taming of the Shrew* has increasingly come to seem one of Shakespeare's more problematic comedies – a play, like *The Merchant of Venice* or *Measure for Measure*, whose ending leaves one with unresolved concerns about the prevailing structure of power. Twentieth-century critical interpretation tends to focus heavily on the marriage of Katherina and Petruchio, with critics grappling in all sorts of ways with how one might understand a show-stopping speech in which the previously subversive woman voices her own submission.

A review of criticism is usefully shaped by identifying three broad approaches to the taming plot. There are the readings that interpret Katherina's and Petruchio's partnership as an expression of love typical, for example, of romantic comedy; there are the readings that locate the action within an early modern historical moment, presenting it as a form of overt ideological display; and there are the 'trickster' readings that argue through analysis, for example, of irony and theatricality that the play only *seems* to affirm male privilege and female subjection.

Love, Games and Marriage

Critics who interpret the taming action in terms of romantic comedy find in Katherina's and Petruchio's evolving relationship a celebration of marriage and mutuality. '[O]nly a very dull reader,' Sir Arthur Quiller-Couch notes in his 1928 introduction, 'can miss recognising [Katherina], under her froward mask, as one of Shakespeare's women, marriageable and willing to mate' (2002, p. 43). Shakespeare's mature comedies – *Much Ado About Nothing*, in particular, with its fiery and dynamic lovers, determined not to marry – are frequently taken as the ultimate artistic treatment of this early sketch. Katherina, according to this line of argument, is less 'crush[ed] . . .

into cowed submission' than brought to a 'full realisation of her potentialities as a woman' (Wells, 1980, p. 59). The assumption is that Katherina begins the play 'a very troubled woman' (Heilman, 1966, p. 156), and is slowly taught by Petruchio how to interact with others in a more personally fulfilling and rewarding manner.

The difficult question, of course, is how one defines 'fulfilling', and whether (and why) she should be forced to conform to Petruchio's ideal of wifely behaviour. Criticism of *The Shrew* is sometimes marred by unexamined and limiting political attitudes to women's role in the home and society. Charles Brooks, for example, finds Katherina learning how to bring her supposedly natural capacity for 'male dominance and female submission' into a balance appropriate for marriage: 'Every woman, then, has within her both a need to submit and a will to dominate, and the harmony of the character depends on the balance between the two. . . . Shakespeare's point would seem to be that . . . it is perhaps healthier to burn out the male through such experience as . . . Kate's than to let it rest dormant and suddenly flare forth as it does with Bianca' (1960, p. 353). Michael West, by contrast, reads the play as an affirmation of sexuality, arguing that 'criticism has generally misconstrued the issue of the play as women's rights, whereas what the audience delightedly responds to are sexual rites' (1974, p. 71). West is too quick, however, to assume that all women 'naturally' aspire to heterosexual sex within the institution of marriage when he asserts that Katherine, 'a healthy female animal', 'wants a male strong enough to protect her, deflower her, and sire vigorous offspring' (p. 69). Quiller-Couch's coy discussion of the continued prevalence in his own day of 'scolding' women implicitly establishes with the (male) reader an 'us and them' opposition, making it apparent that his sympathy as a (male) critic rests primarily with those who have to suffer under the burden of a noisy wife: 'Petruchio's [way of dealing with a shrew] was undoubtedly drastic and has gone out of fashion. But . . . one cannot help thinking a little wistfully that the Petruchian discipline had something to say for itself' (2002, p. 43).

These essentialist attitudes about male and female marital roles are often tempered by the argument that Katherina's behaviour is not only troublesome to her family and neighbours, but destructive to her own well-being. Katherina thus benefits, rather than loses, from her experiences with Petruchio. A powerful and widespread metaphorical reading sees their relationship as an initiation into games, Petruchio teaching Katherina how to embrace life and love through play. For Marianne L. Novy, 'the game element in the *Shrew*', especially when understood in the context of changing attitudes towards marriage in Renaissance England, 'sets up a protected space where imagination permits the enjoyment of both energy and form, while the dangers of violence, tyranny, deadening submission, and resentment magically disappear' (1984, p. 279).

An important and recurrent aspect of the research on the function of games in *The Shrew* is their ability to disrupt numbing convention. J. Dennis Huston compares a capacity for spontaneous invention to theatrical improvisation, arguing that Petruchio provides the disruptive, unpredictable force able to free Katherina from an otherwise mechanical existence:

> [I]n a world ruled, not served, by convention, energies once sponta-
> neously felt either dissolve into cliché – Baptista talking like a loving
> father about his daughters, Lucentio pining after Bianca in the language
> of a Renaissance sonneteer, Hortensio fitting his love poetry to the
> formula of a gamut – or lock themselves into obsessive, repetitious
> behavior – Grumio's recurrent concern for food and sex, Gremio's
> instinctive twitch toward his money bag, Kate's repeated attempts to beat
> others into submission. In such a world man is threatened ultimately by
> dehumanization . . . he cannot *act* in the true philosophical or theatrical
> sense of the word because he can no longer feel. All spontaneity, all play
> disappears . . . Petruchio calls Kate out of the woodenness of the puppet
> show into the human theater of play. Her answer is, shortly, to command
> stage-center.   (1981, pp. 84–5)

The lord in the Induction, Petruchio, and eventually Katherina share 'a special vision, an awareness of life as a play or a game, that gives them a power to control not only their own lives but other people's' (Leggatt, 1974, p. 62).

For these critics, the moment when Katharina enters into Petruchio's spirit of play is usually identified as occurring in the sun–moon scene (IV.v). As Stanley Wells puts it, 'There is a new-found articulacy in Kate's style here [IV.v.16–22]; and is there not something of a dig, not wholly submissive, at Petruchio in "the moon changes even as your mind"? . . . [The following episode with Vincentio] reveals Kate not merely concurring with her husband in patent absurdity, but entering with full imaginative commitment into what now seems more like a game than a display of the results of brain-washing' (1980, pp. 58–9). Katherina not only confirms her husband's (false) perception, but adapts to it her own expansive creativity, playing exuberant riffs on the sun as moon, and Vincentio as a '[y]oung budding virgin'. This lightness of touch, as Alexander Leggatt and John C. Bean remind us (1974, p. 59; 1980, p. 73), is missing from the anonymous *Taming of a Shrew*, where its parallel scene culminates in a less than joyous threat delivered by Ferando (Petruchio) to his obedient wife:

> I am glad, Kate, your stomach is come down.
> I know it well thou knowest it is the sun,
> But I did try to see if thou wouldst speak,
> And cross me now as thou hast done before.
> And trust me, Kate, hadst thou not named the moon,
> We had gone back again as sure as death (E4ᵛ).

Katherina's final speech, as interpreted by those who celebrate her ability finally to embrace a spirit of play, is her moment of 'victory' (Huston, 1981, p. 78; Heilman, 1966, p. 160):

> [T]he very nature of Kate's performance *as* performance suggests that she is offering herself to Petruchio not as his servant, as she claims, but as his equal in a select society which includes themselves, the playwright, and perhaps a few members of his audience: those who, because they know that man is an actor, freely choose and change their roles in order to avoid the narrow, imprisoning roles society would impose on them. (Huston, 1981, p. 78)

The speech is not ironic, then, but neither has Katherina's spirit been beaten down. On the contrary, she 'is simply enjoying herself' (Leggatt, 1974, p. 61), 'it is *her* scene, dominated, and in large measure defined, by her major speech in the play' (Huston, 1981, p. 78).

Moreover, comparison of the substance of Katherina's speech as it appears in Shakespeare's version and in the anonymous play (see Chapter 3, pp. 109–10) shows how Shakespeare has adapted his material. He embeds in her speech 'not a rehearsal of old, medieval ideas about wives but of relatively contemporary ideas growing out of humanist reforms': 'Male tyranny . . . gives way here to a nontyrannical hierarchy informed by mutual affection' (Bean, 1980, p. 70).

A ready point of comparison with the taming plot is provided by the extended courtship of the younger sister, Bianca. This romantic intrigue plot depends for its success on the familiar devices of multiple suitors, disguised identities, Petrarchan love imagery, and obstacles to young love, particularly in the form of a blocking father figure. Greer develops a sustained analysis of Katherina and Bianca as differently deserving types of woman, presenting the latter as 'the soul of duplicity, married without earnestness or good will' (1980, p. 206). Leggatt locates the importance of the romance plot in its very conventionality, in the way it foregrounds the singular achievement of Katherina and Petruchio: 'Both socially and artistically, [Lucentio] has won a conventional sweetheart in a conventional way; and when the prize turns out to have been a baited trap, not merely the character but the conventions he has operated under are mocked' (1974, p. 48).

Readings that find Katherina and Petruchio arriving at a mutually rewarding accommodation seek to celebrate the institution of marriage as 'addition, not subtraction' (Daniell, 1984, p. 30). What is less often noted, however, is that it is not marriage, but a particular vision of marriage that the love and mutuality readings are prepared to ratify, since these critics tend to agree with Petruchio that Lucentio and Hortensio are 'sped'. Paradoxically, a recognition of the final scene's decidedly partial treatment of marital joy only confirms, rather than disrupts, the comic resolution, with Bianca and the Widow becoming the sullen foils to Katherina's sparkling success. Marital unconventionality and originality is commended, but evidently only under certain (i.e., Petruchio's) conditions. This blindspot or ideological prejudice perhaps says more for a highly theatricalized juxtaposition of obedient and disobedient wives and Shakespeare's adept manipulation of stagecraft and comic form than for what Greer calls the playwright's 'theory of marriage' (1980, p. 206).

Advocates of Katherina's marriage occasionally stumble at the brutality of Petruchio's taming methods, especially when they find themselves forced to act as reluctant apologists for it. This material, as Jan Harold Brunvald's meticulous study of the shrew-taming folk-tale tradition indicates, is formulaic. The closest analogue in English to Shakespeare's plot is an anonymous ballad, published around 1550, called 'A Merry Jest of a Shrewd and Curst Wife Lapped in Morel's Skin, for Her Good Behaviour' (see Chapter 3). In the ballad, a wilfull wife is beaten in a cellar by her frustrated husband until she promises to obey his commands. Shakespeare is thus sometimes commended for the way he handles his source material, transform-ing physical into psychological torture. However, as Linda Woodbridge dryly notes, this hardly counts as progressive feminist politics: 'to my mind, it does not speak well of a hero that the best thing to be said in his favor is that he neither beats his wife senseless nor wraps her in a salted horsehide' (1984, p. 207). Charles Marowitz, in the introduction to the published script of his theatrical treatment of Shakespeare's play, underscores the point that '[t]he modern tech-nique for brainwashing is, almost to the letter, what Petruchio makes Katherine undergo' (1990, p. 18). Rather than render acceptable such brutality through recourse to an ideology of love, Marowitz trans-forms Petruchio's '[v]ictory' (Seronsy, 1963, p. 23) into 'the artificially induced spectacle of a mesmerized or drugged victim droning the words her tormentors could not make her speak voluntarily' (1990, p. 19; see also Chapter 4, p. 130).

Bean concedes that The Shrew, in which Katherina is 'depersonal-ize[d]' by 'the unassimilated elements of farce', is 'more primitive' than the mature comedies (1980, p. 75). But Robert B. Heilman, using metaphors of slavery to represent a world of gender criticism turned upside down, condemns the way '[w]e have domesticated a free-swinging farce and made it into . . . the voice of a woman's world in which apron strings, while proclaiming themselves the gentle badge of duty, snap like an overseer's lash' (1966, p. 151). Heilman's view is that there is no 'real' brutality in The Shrew. The play is a farce and so, in the manner of a Wile E. Coyote who falls in

Loony-Toon cartoons from great heights or picks up exploding bombs only to continue the chase in one piece in the next episode, Katherina bounces back from her experiences with Petruchio unscathed:

> Farce offers a spectacle that resembles daily actuality but lets us partici-
> pate without feeling the responsibilities and liabilities that the situation
> would normally evoke . . . Farce is the realm without pain or conscience.
> Farce offers a holiday from vulnerability, consequences, costs. It is the
> opposite of all the dramas of disaster in which a man's fate is too much
> for him. It carries out our persistent if unconscious desire to simplify life
> by a selective anaesthetizing of the whole person; in farce, man retains all
> his energy yet never gets really hurt.   (p. 152)

This discussion of literary genre is usefully contextualized through consideration of the play's fortunes on the stage, particularly in the eighteenth and nineteenth centuries when farce and slapstick gags dominated theatrical interpretation (see Chapter 4, pp. 120–7).

Petruchio's taming methods are reconciled only with difficulty to a view of romantic love. Not even Hugh Richmond's diagnosis of Katherina as a 'neurotic', 'suffer[ing] from an unthinking fascination with courtship and love, the lack of which is driving her nearly to frenzy' (1971, p. 86), can banish entirely critical reservations that she is deprived of food, sleep and creature comforts, not ultimately for her own benefit or 'cure', but for her husband's ease (for a filmic version of the taming plot as 'therapy', see Chapter 4, pp. 131–6). Emily Detmer, insisting on the very real and damaging effects of psychological coercion, argues that Katherina's eventual identification with her husband's will is typical of the Stockholm Syndrome, a condition which finds victims of domestic violence bonding with their persecutor(s) in return for even small kindnesses. Detmer, Marowitz and Woodbridge resist still-prevalent cultural and critical assumptions that the experience of marriage can be loving or plea-surable for Katherina as an abused wife. They do so, however, at the price of not finding anything at all comic in this early Shakespearean comedy.

Reading Old Books

Perhaps this comedy is irredeemably of its time, and it is a mistake to try to 'save' Shakespeare by finding in *The Shrew* either romantic love or progressive attitudes to male–female relations. This is the insight provided by critics who value 'the unequivocality with which the play locates both women's abjected position in the social order of early modern England and the costs exacted for resistance' (Boose, 1991, p. 179). Lynda E. Boose attempts to recover 'the real village Kates who underwrite Shakespeare's character' (p. 181) by unearthing historical and antiquarian scholarship on cucking and bridling. Her study of the practice of fitting women accused of unruly behaviour with a painful metal bit and parading them through the streets, or tying them to a chair and immersing them repeatedly in water makes for chilling reading, and sheds a salutary perspective on the ideological significance of Petruchio's assertion of 'right supremacy' (V.ii.108). Gary Schneider argues that *The Shrew* enacts a similarly public shaming strategy (at Katherina's wedding, and elsewhere), before dramatizing in the fourth act a private process of 'mortification' defined by an 'ethic of asceticism' (2002, p. 249). In the final scene, ' "Kate" is less a character within the play than a spokesperson of a very patriarchal rhetoric . . . [her] speech is a *public* spectacle that concludes a process of temporal behavior; in short, the speech buttresses the civilizing process by acting as an *exemplum* to Bianca, to the Widow, and to the (female) playgoers' (pp. 251–2).

An interest in the early modern household shapes a number of historically oriented studies. Lena Cowen Orlin adopts an anthropological perspective on the various uses of things, and people as things, to argue that the goods talked about in the play or seen on stage ground 'the prevailing power relationship between men and women' in contractual terms (1993, p. 187). In a chapter consistent with critical perspectives that celebrate the play's discovery of mutuality within marriage, John Russell Brown argues that Petruchio from the outset displays emotional and financial generosity, eventually teaching this openness to Katherina. A focus on women's education prompts Natasha Korda to reach very different conclusions about Petruchio's liberality. Bianca and Katherina, as Brown and others have long recognized, are taught very differently and to different effect by their suitor-tutors. Korda discerns in this the emergence of an economic order in which the housewife has to learn how to advance her husband's symbolic credit without breaking him financially – a lesson Katherina, but not Bianca, is forced to internalize by the end of the play. A perception of generosity is likewise challenged by Lynda E. Boose who situates the parallel marriage plots in relation to the changing material and economic circumstances of Elizabethan property ownership. Boose reads Petruchio's meteoric rise from 'a needy wanderer to the bed of a highborn wife' (1994, p. 224) as 'the fantasy of a bourgeois (male) culture', 'a paradigm of the success story of the English yeomanry' (p. 216, see also Chapter 3, pp. 112–16, for documents from the period on property law and marriage).

It was the opinion of C. S. Lewis that *The Shrew* embodies attitudes that will inevitably jar with modern political sensibilities. His response, however, is decidedly, almost comically, unapologetic as he inveighs against 'modern producers' who, 'failing to accept [Shakespeare's] notion of natural authority', encourage a 'tactical or ironical' reading of Katherina's submission:

> There is not a hint of this in the lines Shakespeare has given her. If we ask what Katharina's submission forebodes, I think Shakespeare has given us his answer through the lips of Petruchio: 'Marry, peace it bodes, and love and quiet life, An awful rule and right supremacy, And, to be short, what not, that's sweet and happy?' The words, thus taken at their face value, are very startling to a modern audience; but those who cannot face such startling should not read old books. (1956, pp. 74–5)

'Lump it or leave it', one might paraphrase in the colloquial. Nearly fifty years later, Shirley Nelson Garner chooses to leave it. For Garner, *The Shrew* evinces little interest apart from marking a particular historical moment both in Shakespeare's career and in traditions of misogynist attitudes toward women: 'As someone who does not share [its patriarchal] values, I find much of the play humorless. . . . If I went to see it, it would be out of curiosity, to find out how someone in our time would direct it' (1988, pp. 117–18). Anecdotally, at least, it would appear that Garner is not alone in her opinion, since it is not unusual to hear theatre-goers freely admit that their preferred way of

dealing with *The Shrew* is to avoid it altogether. And yet, paradoxically, it remains in the theatre one of the most frequently revived of
Shakespeare's comedies (see Chapter 4).

The problem with old-style historicist, new historicist, and mate-
rialist feminist readings of *The Shrew*, insightful though these analyses
of the text can be, is that they often fail to transfer to the modern
stage. 'History', as W. B. Worthen has made us aware, is always in
performance an *effect* of 'pastness' created through the manipulation
of available – and always very modern – materials, bodies and behaviours. Therefore even a treatment of Shakespeare's drama, historically accurate in all its details, is never of a temporally and culturally
distant world, but of an audience's own present moment, the performance continually slipping into its moment of enactment.

Hearing Irony

The appeal to some readers and spectators of a third set of responses
to the taming plot – the trickster readings – is that they resist a patriarchal social order while yet allowing for the possibility of comic
energy by arguing that Katherina only *seems* to conform to her
husband's will. In terms of performance, one thinks here of Mary
Pickford's broad wink to the camera in the 1929 film version (see
Chapter 4, pp. 126–7), or of theatrical versions that undercut the moralizing of Katherina's final speech through such devices as the addition
of an epilogue or the insertion of comic stage business such as cuckold's horns descending from the flies to rest over the head of an
unwitting Petruchio as Katherina preaches the obedience that wives
owe their husbands. While popular in the theatre, this interpretation
has attracted variable critical reaction. Objections to hearing irony in
Katherina's final speech include accusations of anachronism (Lewis),
a lack of textual basis for supposing that she does not mean what she
says (Saccio, 1984, p. 39), the view that 'some forty lines of straight
irony would be too much to be borne' (Heilman, 1966, p. 159), a desire
to find 'a special quality of mutuality' between Katherina and
Petruchio, 'sealed for them both by Kate's last speech' (Daniell, 1984,
p. 28), and the assertion that 'turn[ing] Kate back into a hidden shrew

whose new technique was sarcastic indirection, side-mouthing at the audience while her not very intelligent husband, bamboozled, cheered her on . . . would be a poor triumph' (Heilman, 1966, p. 159).

Games, evidently, constitute lighthearted fun only when the husband plays them with, and on, his wife, not when the wife plays them on her husband. The arguments commonly cited in favour of an ironic interpretation of Katherina's final speech grow out of what Coppélia Kahn describes as the 'dramatic context':

> It fairly shouts obedience, when a gentle murmur would suffice. . . . Second, though the speech pleads subordination, as a speech – a lengthy, ambitious verbal performance before an audience – it allows the speaker to dominate that audience. . . . Third, the speech sets the seal on a complete reversal of character, a push-button change from rebel to conformist which is, I have argued, part of the mechanism of farce. Here as elsewhere in the play, farce has two purposes: it completes the fantasy of male dominance, but also mocks it as mere fantasy. (1981, p. 99)

The very circumstances within which the speech is staged, in other words, encourage us to hear irony, whether or not one wishes in addition to argue that Katherina has fallen in love with her master (a prospect Kahn sees as 'quite possibl[e]'). Wayne A. Rebhorn, documenting the unease generated historically by rhetoricians' 'slippery' ability 'to create civic order or foment rebellion' (1995, p. 325), argues that Katherina hones not her obedience but her power of oratory: 'she is the same Katherine at the end of the play that she was at the beginning, just as Christopher Sly, no matter how nobly dressed and waited upon, remains irreducibly himself in his every appearance' (p. 324). In the final scene, 'authorize[d]' by her husband 'to play the orator' (p. 327), Katherine 'deconstruct[s] the right rule/tyranny opposition maintained within the discourse of rhetoric':

> [I]f the speech supports Petruchio's desire to justify his position as a loving sovereign motivated by care for the well-being of his subjects [lines 135–63], it also suggests that such a positive identification can never entirely eliminate its negative counterpart and prevent the loving sovereign from appearing a brutal tyrant who coerces, bullies, drags, invades, and rapes his subject into submission [lines 164–78]. Read in this way,

Katherine's speech subverts where otherwise it seems to confirm the social order. Or perhaps it would be better to say that it may subvert this order, for there is no necessary reason why the two parts of the speech must be read one way or the other.   (p. 326)

The irony is therefore not just contextual, as Kahn argues, but built into the very structure of the speech with which Katherina ostensibly subjects herself to her husband. The silence of Bianca and the Widow may suggest they remain unconvinced by either the nature of Katherina's wifely obedience or the rhetorical form it takes. As Rebhorn suggests, reading and theatre audiences have to make up their own minds.

The debate about irony in *The Shrew* is likely to run and run. The problem (and beauty) of this early comedy is the way it remains open to endless, even conflicting, interpretation, yet prompts in many spectators and readers an intense ideological investment in gender roles, both as played out in Shakespeare's time and our own. For those who wish to control audience reception of the action – whether as a positive affirmation of patriarchal systems of power or as a feminist resistance to them – *The Taming of the Shrew* is bound to frustrate. 'Since the actor and the character can never coalesce', as Barry Weller perceptively notes, '[Katherina's] emotions are by definition untrue' (1992, p. 322). But in the case of a politically inflammatory play such as *The Shrew*, this 'uncertainty . . . protects it from reductiveness' (p. 323).

Reading the drama metatheatrically – as a play that presents itself in various ways as 'just a play' – is a powerful critical means to undercut the perceived severity of the taming narrative without relinquishing altogether the play's comic potential. Weller's discussion of irony and theatre grows out of an extensive analysis of the multiple levels at which the action of *The Shrew* overtly manipulates ideas of real and feigned identity. The play has a tripartite structure embracing the induction, taming plot and romantic comedy intrigue, with pretense and role-play – what Cecil Seronsy identifies as the 'supposes' theme – linking each of these separate threads. In such a highly and fluidly theatricalized context, where audiences become the spectacle and actors the onstage audience, it can be difficult to determine with precision who is performing, when, and for whom – with the result that any firm conclusion about whether Katherina in the final scene merely play-acts the obedient wife necessarily recedes into indeterminacy.

The play's self-conscious theatricality likewise raises issues about other potential ways the three plots might be seen to intersect. In particular, is Petruchio best identified with the Induction's lord, two male characters in positions of power who impose new identities on the socially vulnerable (women and tinkers), or does he most resemble the shape-shifter, Sly? Jayne Sears, provocatively, if somewhat fancifully, imagines a production in which Sly falls asleep and dreams he plays the part of Petruchio, only to wake up at the end and, in a manner not dissimilar to Bottom in *A Midsummer Night's Dream*, 'try to puzzle out his dream in a comic pantomime' (1966, p. 43). Treatment of the inset narrative as a sort of wish-fulfilment, as 'a childish dream of omnipotence' (Kahn, 1981, p. 85), has proven popular in performance as it imposes a distance between the inset play and the theatre audience, encouraging a critical aloofness from what is staged in one way or another as Sly's, rather than the spectators' own, fantasy (see Chapter 4, pp. 137–9).

Rather than explain this distancing effect in terms of irony, or as a particular character's dream, Michael Shapiro traces the way the theatre audience is made aware that the 'women' in question are really male actors playing 'idealized married gentlewomen or their unruly antitypes' – theatrical constructions, certainly, but also stereotypes of femininity 'as outlined in conduct books and marriage manuals' (1993, p. 144). Investigations of theatricality and gender constructionism frequently seek in some way to recuperate the drama's politics. Karen Newman, like Shapiro, argues that the ideological force of Katherina's final speech is undermined by the way the play 'call[s] attention to the constructed character of the representation' (1991, p. 42). Holly A. Crocker suggests that Katherina, finally learning that female passivity and submission are attributes that can be measured only in relation to the behaviour of other women, ultimately escapes her husband's agency: 'by *taking on* the ideology of femininity that Petruchio promotes, she *takes from* Petruchio the feminine submission he purports to desire . . . Katharine's pose of submission, which must be at once sincere and artificial, is thus the most destabilizing aspect of the play (2003, p. 156). As Kahn notes, however, the problem with readings that locate empowerment in Katherina's performance – in a female voice that changes its tune but not its stridency – is that '[t]hough Kate is clever enough to use his verbal strategies against him, she is trapped in her own cleverness. Her only way of maintaining her inner freedom is by outwardly denying it, which thrusts her into a schizoid existence' (1981, p. 96).

Shapiro, Newman and Crocker find at least the potential for a liberating view of gender relations since a constructionist model of identity implicitly admits of change. Such essays tend to argue, further, that the stylized action of *The Shrew* sufficiently presents Katherina's submission 'as the final incarnation of an elaborately but transparently constructed ideal of upperclass femininity' (Shapiro, 1993, p. 166), without any need to return to the Sly plot in the closing moments to highlight the play's in-built theatricality.

Richard A. Burt, countering claims that layers of artifice and role-play are plainly evident in the final scene, yet taking issue with scholars who find in the play a celebration of love and marriage, works through a constructionist argument at the level of the theatre audience. It is we, not the character of Katherina, who are worked on to believe that male coercion of female will is acceptable – beneficial, even – by the way the play conceals inflexible power structures behind a 'enchant[ing]' (1984, p. 306) smokescreen of romantic love. Burt's discussion of ideological manipulation accounts for Sly's non-appearance, not as redundant and so unnecessary, but as 'symptomatic of the play's social function': 'were the frame to return, it would jeopardize the social function of the comedy . . . [B]y suggesting that the play is only a dream, only a play-within-a-play, the frame would heighten our sense of the artificiality of Petruchio's behavior at the very moment the play is at pains to naturalize it' (pp. 305–6). Yet another way to account for the open-endedness of the Sly frame is to interpret the action as on-going. '[I]f Sly's story is not over', as Margie Burns argues, 'perhaps Kate and Petruchio's is not over either. Their wedding occurred back in Act III, after all, so the audience knows that a wedding does not necessarily signify closure any more than it necessarily signifies the happy ending. . . . For Kate and Petruchio, the open ending is the most persuasive happy ending, because the open threshold promises them room to grow' (1986, p. 55). Joel Fineman, studying how woman is situated as 'the embodiment of difference' (1985, p. 153) in an essay indebted to Derridean and Lacanian language play, suggests that Sly's absence speaks to this condition of otherness and indeterminacy: the audience is left 'with a desire for closure that the play calls forth in order to postpone' (p. 156).

Comedy and Controversy

Finding a way to play *The Shrew* as comic in the modern theatre is one of the greatest challenges to confront twenty-first century directors and actors. Playing it 'straight' can seem merely to affirm sexist values, both of Shakespeare's time and our own, an interpretation that many spectators – male and female – no longer find amusing. Yet to make Katherina's transformation seem unduly ironic or to call attention to Petruchio's brutality or Baptista's callousness is to transform Shakespeare's play from farcical comedy into light tragedy.

But perhaps it is a mistake to assume that our task is to recover in performance (a term that can embrace both theatre and criticism) the play's 'original' humour. We in fact have precious little information about how *The Shrew* was received in its earliest stagings and by its earliest critics, and what we do know is ambiguous, at best. John Harington ironically wrote in 1596 in the *Metamorphosis of Ajax*, in a comment that could easily apply to Shakespeare's version of the story, 'For the shrewd wife, read the book of Taming a Shrew, which hath made a number of us so perfect, that now every one can rule a shrew in our country, save he that hath her.'

John Fletcher, a playwright who collaborated with Shakespeare on *Henry VIII* and *The Two Noble Kinsmen*, wrote a sequel to *The Shrew* in 1611, called *The Woman's Prize, or The Tamer Tamed*. This comedy opens after the death of Katherina, with Petruchio marrying the chaste Maria, a woman who, refusing to be tamed in the manner of her predecessor, resolves that 'I'll make you know, and fear a wife, Petruchio'. What follows is a series of slapstick episodes in which

Maria frustrates Petruchio at every turn. When they are eventually reconciled, Petruchio forgivingly, even proudly, concludes, 'Well, little England, when I see a husband / Of any other nation, stern or jealous, / I'll wish him but a woman of thy breeding'. When these two plays were performed before the king and queen in 1633, the Master of the Revels (Henry Herbert), noted that Shakespeare's play was 'Liked', but Fletcher's was 'Very well liked' (Morris, 1981, pp. 88–9). This surviving reception history suggests that *The Shrew* and its gender politics might well have been regarded in its own time as controversial. It has become commonplace to note that one never encounters Shakespeare in a political vacuum. Inevitably, critical and theatrical reception of *The Shrew* is determined by a lens fashioned by a shifting cultural landscape, a landscape defined, not least, by inter-sections of sex and power.

Bibliography

Modern Editions and Anthologies

Aspinall, Dana (ed.), *The Taming of the Shrew: Critical Essays* (London: Routledge, 2002). Samples a history of the play's critical reception.

Aughterson, Kate, *Renaissance Woman: A Sourcebook* (London: Routledge, 1995). An excellent collection of sermons, conduct books and polemical tracts from the sixteenth and seventeenth centuries relating to women.

Bloom, Harold (ed.), *William Shakespeare's 'The Taming of the Shrew'* (New York: Chelsea House, 1988). Reprints eight slightly dated, but nonetheless key, essays on the play.

Dolan, Frances E. (ed.), *The Taming of the Shrew: Texts and Contexts* (Boston, MA: Bedford Books, 1996). Handy collection of documents that are of relevance especially to questions of domestic hierarchies, service and marriage. Extracts are reprinted alongside a text of the play edited by David Bevington.

Hibbard, G. R. (ed.), *The Taming of the Shrew*, with a new Introduction by Margaret Jane Kidnie, New Penguin Shakespeare (London: Penguin, 2005).

Marvel, Laura (ed.), *Readings on 'The Taming of the Shrew'* (San Diego: Greenhaven Press, 2000). Reprints extracts from key critical essays, thematically organized.

Morris, Brian (ed.), *The Taming of the Shrew*, Arden Shakespeare (London: Routledge, 1981). Reliable text and full introduction.

Oliver, H. J. (ed.), *The Taming of the Shrew*, Oxford Shakespeare (Oxford: Oxford University Press, 1982). Reliable text and full introduction.

Thompson, Ann (ed.), *The Taming of the Shrew*, New Cambridge Shakespeare (Cambridge: Cambridge University Press, 1984). Reliable text and full introduction.

Wynne-Davies, Marion (ed.), '*Much Ado About Nothing*' and '*The Taming of the Shrew*', New Casebooks series (Basingstoke: Palgrave, 2001). Reprints five outstanding essays on *The Shrew*.

Textual and Source Studies

Brunvand, Jan Harold, 'The Folktale Origin of *The Taming of the Shrew*', *Shakespeare Quarterly* 17 (1966): 345–59.

Hosley, Richard, 'Was there a "Dramatic Epilogue" to *The Taming of the Shrew*?', *Studies in English Literature, 1500–1900* 1:2 (1961): 17–34.

Marcus, Leah, *Unediting the Renaissance: Shakespeare, Milton, Marlowe* (London: Routledge, 1996). A feminist analysis of *A Shrew*, *The Shrew*, and the editorial tradition.

Miller, Stephen (ed.), *The Taming of a Shrew*, The Early Quartos (Cambridge: Cambridge University Press, 1988). Full modernized text of the anonymous play.

——, '*The Taming of a Shrew* and the Theories; or, "Though this be badness, yet there is method in't."' *Textual Formations and Reformations*, ed. Laurie E. Maguire and Thomas L. Berger (1998): 251–63. A very readable comparison of *A Shrew* and *The Shrew*, and the theories devised to account for their similarities and differences.

Wells, Stanley and Gary Taylor, with John Jowett and William Montgomery, *William Shakespeare: A Textual Companion* (Oxford: Oxford University Press, 1988). An excellent brief summary of the play's textual problems.

Critical Reception

[*Cross-references to anthologies provided where available.*]

Bean, John C., 'Comic Structure and the Humanizing of Kate in *The Taming of the Shrew*', *The Woman's Part: Feminist Criticism of*

Shakespeare, ed. Carolyn Ruth Swift Lenz, Gayle Greene and Carol Thomas Neely (Urbana: University of Illinois Press, 1980), pp. 65–78. See Marvel.

Boose, Lynda E., 'Scolding Brides and Bridling Scolds: Taming the Woman's Unruly Member', *Shakespeare Quarterly* 42 (1991): 179–213. See Aspinall; Wynne-Davies.

——, 'The Taming of the Shrew, Good Husbandry, and Enclosure', *Shakespeare Reread: The Texts in New Contexts*, ed. Russ McDonald (Ithaca, NY: Cornell University Press, 1994), pp. 193–225. See Marvel.

Brooks, Charles, 'Shakespeare's Romantic Shrews', *Shakespeare Quarterly* 11 (1960): 351–6.

Brown, John Russell, *Shakespeare and His Comedies* (1957; London: Methuen, 1968).

Burns, Margie, 'The Ending of *The Shrew*', *Shakespeare Studies* 18 (1986): 41–64. See Aspinall.

Burt, Richard A., 'Charisma, Coercion, and Comic Form in *The Taming of the Shrew*', *Criticism* 26 (1984): 295–311. See Bloom.

Crocker, Holly A., 'Affective Resistance: Performing Passivity and Playing A-Part in *The Taming of the Shrew*', *Shakespeare Quarterly* 54.2 (2003): 142–59.

Daniell, David, 'The Good Marriage of Katherina and Petruchio', *Shakespeare Survey* 37 (1984): 23–31. See Aspinall.

Detmer, Emily, 'Civilizing Subordination: Domestic Violence and *The Taming of the Shrew*', *Shakespeare Quarterly* 48 (1997): 273–94. See Marvel.

Fineman, Joel, 'The Turn of the Shrew', *Shakespeare and the Question of Theory*, ed. Patricia Parker and Geoffrey Hartman (New York: Methuen, 1985), 138–59. See Bloom; Wynne-Davies.

Garner, Shirley Nelson, '*The Taming of the Shrew*: Inside or Outside of the Joke?', *'Bad' Shakespeare: Revaluations of the Shakespeare Canon*, ed. Maurice Charney (Rutherford: Fairleigh Dickinson University Press, 1988), pp. 105–19.

Greer, Germaine, *The Female Eunuch* (1971; New York: McGraw-Hill Paperback, 1980).

Heilman, Robert B., 'The *Taming* Untamed, or, The Return of the Shrew', *Modern Language Quarterly* 27 (1966): 147–61. See Marvel.

Huston, J. Dennis, *Shakespeare's Comedies of Play* (New York: Columbia University Press, 1981). See Marvel.

Kahn, Coppelia, *Man's Estate: Masculine Identity in Shakespeare* (Berkeley, CA: University of California Press, 1981). See Bloom.

Korda, Natasha, *Shakespeare's Domestic Economies: Gender and Property in Early Modern England* (Philadelphia: University of Pennsylvania Press, 2002). See Aspinall; Wynne-Davies.

Leggatt, Alexander, *Shakespeare's Comedy of Love* (London: Methuen, 1974).

Lewis, C. S., *A Preface to Paradise Lost* (1942; London: Oxford University Press, 1956).

Newman, Karen, *Fashioning Femininity and English Renaissance Drama* (Chicago: University of Chicago Press, 1991). See Wynne-Davies.

Novy, Marianne L., *Love's Argument: Gender Relations in Shakespeare* (Chapel Hill: University of North Carolina Press, 1984). See Bloom.

Orlin, Lena Cowen, 'The Performance of Things in *The Taming of the Shrew*', *Yearbook of English Studies* 23 (1993): 167–88. See Aspinall.

Quiller-Couch, Sir Arthur, 'From his Introduction to *The Taming of the Shrew* (1928). In *The Taming of the Shrew: Critical Essays*, ed. Dana E. Aspinall (London: Routledge, 2002) pp. 41–4.

Rebhorn, Wayne A., 'Petruchio's "Rope Tricks": "The Taming of the Shrew" and the Renaissance Discourse of Rhetoric', *Modern Philology* 92 (1995): 294–327.

Richmond, Hugh, *Shakespeare's Sexual Comedy: A Mirror for Lovers* (New York: Bobbs-Merrill, 1971).

Saccio, Peter, 'Shrewd and Kindly Farce', *Shakespeare Survey* 37 (1984): 33–40.

Schneider, Gary, 'The Public, the Private, and the Shaming of the Shrew', *Studies in English Literature, 1500–1900* 42 (2002): 235–52.

Seronsy, Cecil C., ' "Supposes" as the Unifying Theme in *The Taming of the Shrew*', *Shakespeare Quarterly* 14 (1963): 15–30.

Shapiro, Michael, 'Framing the Taming: Metahistorical Awareness of Female Impersonation in *The Taming of the Shrew*', *Yearbook of English Studies* 23 (1993): 143–66. See Aspinall.

Weller, Barry, 'Induction and Inference: Theater, Transformation, and the Construction of Identity in *The Taming of the Shrew*'. In *Creative*

Imitation: New Essays on Renaissance Literature in Honor of Thomas M. Greene, ed. David Quint, Margaret W. Ferguson, G. W. Pigman III, Wayne A. Rebhorn and Geoffrey Hartman (Binghamton: Medieval and Renaissance Texts and Studies, 1992), pp. 297–329.

Wells, Stanley, '*The Taming of the Shrew* and *King Lear*: A Structural Comparison', *Shakespeare Survey* 33 (1980): 55–66.

West, Michael, 'The Folk Background of Petruchio's Wooing Dance: Male Supremacy in *The Taming of the Shrew*', *Shakespeare Studies* 7 (1974): 65–74. See Marvel.

Woodbridge, Linda, *Women and the English Renaissance: Literature and the Nature of Womankind, 1540–1620* (Urbana: University of Illinois Press, 1984).

Performance and Theatre Studies

Coursen, H. R., *Shakespearean Performance as Interpretation* (London: Associated University Presses, 1992). Argues for a plurality of readings and resists what he terms 'consensus' criticism through analysis of production histories.

Dobson, Michael, *The Making of the National Poet: Shakespeare, Adaptation and Authorship, 1660–1769* (Oxford: Clarendon Press, 1992). Excellent discussion of Garrick's *Catharine and Petruchio*.

Garrick, David, *Catharine and Petruchio: A Comedy, 1756*, vol. 3 of *The Plays of David Garrick*, ed. Harry William Pedicord and Fredrick Louis Bergmann, 3 vols (Carbondale and Edwardsville: Southern Illinois University Press, 1981), pp. 187–220.

Haring-Smith, Tori, *From Farce to Metadrama: A Stage History of 'The Taming of the Shrew', 1594–1983* (Westport, CT: Greenwood Press, 1985). Key reading for analysis of the play in performance.

Henderson, Diane E., 'A Shrew for the Times'. In *Shakespeare, the Movie: Popularizing the Plays on Film, TV, and Video*, ed. Lynda E. Boose and Richard Burt (London: Routledge, 1997), pp. 148–68.

Hodgdon, Barbara, *The Shakespeare Trade: Performances and Appropriations* (Philadelphia: University of Pennsylvania Press, 1998). An astute cultural analysis of bodies and politics in twentieth-century film and theatrical stagings. See Aspinall.

Holderness, Graham, *The Taming of the Shrew*, Shakespeare in Performance Series (Manchester: Manchester University Press, 1989). Analyses of four late-twentieth productions of the play.

Marowitz, Charles, *The Marowitz Shakespeare* (1978; New York: Marion Boyars, 1990).

Miller, Jonathan and Tim Hallinan, 'Interview: Jonathan Miller on the Shakespeare Plays', *Shakespeare Quarterly* 32 (1981): 134–45.

Miller, Jonathan and Graham Holderness, 'Jonathan Miller Interviewed by Graham Holderness'. In *The Shakespeare Myth*, ed. Graham Holderness (Manchester: Manchester University Press, 1988), pp. 195–202.

Rutter, Carol Chillington, 'Looking at Shakespeare's Women on Film'. In *The Cambridge Companion to Shakespeare on Film* (Cambridge: Cambridge University Press, 2000), pp. 241–60. The camera frames particular ideological interpretations of female character.

Schafer, Elizabeth, *The Taming of the Shrew*, Shakespeare in Production Series (Cambridge: Cambridge University Press, 2002). A stage history keyed to Thompson's New Cambridge edition; essential reading for performance-oriented study.

Sears, Jayne, 'The Dreaming of *The Shrew*', *Shakespeare Quarterly* 17 (1966): 41–56.

Shaw, George Bernard, *Shaw on Shakespeare: An Anthology of Bernard Shaw's Writings on the Plays and Production of Shakespeare*, ed. Edwin Wilson (London: Cassell, 1961).

Worthen, W.B. *Shakespeare and the Force of Modern Performance* (Cambridge: Cambridge University Press, 2003).

Film and Television Productions

Kiss Me, Kate, dir. George Sidney, MGM, 1953.

'Moonlighting' – *Shrew* episode, American Broadcasting Company, 1986.

The Taming of the Shrew, dir. Jonathan Miller, BBC–Time/Life, 1980.

The Taming of the Shrew, dir. Sam Taylor, Columbia Pictures, 1929.

The Taming of the Shrew, dir. Franco Zeffirelli, Royal Films International, 1967.

10 Things I Hate About You, dir. Gil Junger, Touchstone Pictures, 1999.

Index